DEER BURGER COOKBOOK

DEER BURGER COOKBOOK

Recipes for Ground Venison—
Soups, Stews, Chilies, Casseroles, Jerkies,
and Sausages

Rick Black

STACKPOLE
BOOKS

Published by
STACKPOLE BOOKS
5067 Ritter Road
Mechanicsburg, PA 17055
www.stackpolebooks.com

Printed in the United States

10 9 8 7 6 5 4 3 2

Cover design by Wendy A. Reynolds

Library of Congress Cataloging-in-Publication Data
Black, Rick.
  Deer burger cookbook : recipes for using ground venison in soups, stews, chilies, casseroles, jerkies, and sausages / Rick Black.—1st ed.
      p. cm.
   Includes index.
   ISBN-13: 978-0-8117-3287-1 (pbk. : alk. paper)
   1. Cookery (Venison) I. Title.

TX751.B56 2006
641.6'91—dc22

                                                                2005022755

ISBN 0-8117-3287-8

I dedicate this book to

My wife, Becky, for putting up with me for over twenty years.

My children, Shaena and Travis, for keeping me young and for being perfect kids.

*My granddaughter, MaKayla, for giving me even more reasons to fish
the beaches of South Carolina.*

*My mom and dad, now deceased, for raising me with Midwestern family values
and giving me the gift of the loved outdoors.*

*And last but not least, you, my loyal readers, who have supported me
and my writings.*

*Without you, Cousin Rick Black would be just another Iowa hunter who loves
telling jokes and trading hunting and fishing tips and tricks.*

CONTENTS

ACKNOWLEDGMENTS

My thanks for help in furnishing data, photos, and for sharing their time, knowledge, and experience go to Mike Hoffman of Keystone; Randy Fox of National Studio; Brad Holland of the Holland Grill Company; the City of Burlington Iowa Parks and Recreation; Chopper's Restaurant; Cosmo of the New Mix 107.3 radio show; Judith Schnell of Stackpole Books; Terry Lee for my computer support; Bill Hayman and Jim Hartschuh of Vista Bakery for support of my writings; and the Iowa Department of Natural Resources.

A special note of thanks also to Amy Lerner for editing the manuscript through all its convolutions with patience and insight and gentle firmness. There are a number of others I'd like to thank, good hunting and fishing companions of years gone by. I only wish they were still here so that I could acknowledge the woods lore lessons they passed on to me, some of which are passed on to you in the following pages.

Finally, I am ever so grateful for the ongoing love and support of my family—Becky, Shaena, and Travis—from whom I've stolen time to work on this project.

R. B.

INTRODUCTION

If you're a dedicated reader of my line of outdoor books, then you know I love hunting. I have had the privilege of hunting with some of the best deer hunters in our United States.

From Minnesota to Texas, and all states in between, when the fall season comes upon us, you will find deer hunters starting to act crazy. We do little things like grunting to oncoming hunters, ordering outfitting magazines, trading videos on tree stand and blind techniques, spending hours at the local sporting goods store pulling back bow strings, cutting our fingers on Brodheads, fumbling around on rifle bolts, shotgun pumps, and trying on the latest and greatest thermocamouflaged clothing. All of this and you can bet that when we arrive at deer camp, someone has forgotten the ammo!

I have found that most deer hunters hunt for three reasons: 1. Sport, the thrill of convenient big-game hunting. 2. The chance of bagging that world record, wall-hanging, lifetime-braggin'-rights monster buck. 3. Good eatin' vittles!

This is where I come in. If I'm not hunting, I'm most likely at a bookstore doing a book signing. And I have been amazed at the number one question I am asked by fellow hunters and their spouses. "Rick, other than jerky and chili, what do I do with all this deer burger?"

That has inspired me to write this book. I want to serve my fellow deer hunters by writing a complete deer burger cookbook. The reader of this book will never again have to ask the question, "What do I do with all this deer burger?"

So let's start at the beginning (for all those greenhorned rookies out there). Remember, you were once a greenhorn too.

PICKING OUT YOUR DEER

If you're meat hunting as opposed to bagging the "wall-hanger," look for a young doe with a nice, chunky, brisket-shaped chest bespeaking plenty of fat. Check the deer for graceful rounding in the hindquarters as well; you will want fat hams, and keep in mind that the rump is where well-fed deer tend to put on padding.

Choose your deer not by size but more so by body conformation that indicates a plump, young, good-tasting meat harvest. A lot of hunters believe that venison fat is rancid; I would guess that these are the hunters that have only cooked with meat from old tough bucks, or a poorly shot animal.

The fresh, white-yellow fat from a well-marbled deer that has been feeding in farmer Brown's corn and bean field is very good tasting food! A good test of how the fat tastes on your deer will be to cut a small piece of fat and fry it. You can immediately tell how this will affect your burger by incorporating it into your meat.

FIELD DRESSING YOUR DEER

It's a dirty job, but someone has to do it! The timely removal of your deer's innards is often necessary to ensure untainted meat, and it also helps reduce the weight you'll have to drag back to your truck or camp. Here is the procedure:

1. If you're in an area that requires tags, tag your deer immediately. The tag must remain with the deer at all times, or you risk dealing with the Fish Cops.
2. Carefully cut a circle around the anus so it's free and can be removed from within. Some hunters tie it off with string to prevent its contents from tainting the meat.
3. If you have a buck, remove and discard the testicles and cut the penis free so that it can be removed the same way as the anus.

4. Beginning close to the pelvis, open the stomach cavity to the rib cage. After starting the cut, use the first two fingers of your free hand to help guide the knife. You must cut only through the skin and a thin layer of meat to avoid the entrails.

5. Cut through the ribs and skin, following the breastbone, up to the neck. This is easy with a good, sharp knife, but don't twist the blade while it's between the bones; a brittle knife blade could easily break if twisted.

6. Continue cutting up to the base of the skull.

7. Sever the windpipe at the base of the skull.

8. Cut the diaphragm loose. (This is the sheet of muscle that separates the stomach area from the chest cavity.)

9. Allow the deer to roll on its side to help the organs to come out. You'll have to pull a little, but they should be mostly free.

10. Be extremely careful in removing the bladder! You must reach up into the pelvis and pinch it shut while you cut it free with the other hand. If any urine is spilled on the meat, remove it immediately with water, snow, or a clean cloth. I always have a five-gallon jug of water back at camp to use as a rinse.

11. Clean any debris from the cavity. Any stomach contents or other substances should be removed as quickly as possible.

12. Separate the heart and liver if you or someone you know likes to eat them. Keep in mind that both make very good burger. I recommend a cloth bag for keeping them clean and allowing them to cool.

13. Start dragging your deer out. If you do not have a quadrunner, or a deer cart, I recommend a plastic sled; they make a big difference on the old back!

MAKING YOUR DEER BURGER

If you really want to know what's in your burger, grind your own. This way you can control the fat content as well as the primal cut. If you're a young buck full of energy and time, an old-fashioned clamp-on galvanized meat grinder still does the trick. If your wife is like mine, then you most likely have a super-duper food processor, and you can make a mess of deer burger in no time!

When using a food processor, cut chunks of venison and fat into one-inch uniform cubes and chill. Place the meat cubes in the processor with metal blade, taking care to process in small batches (no more than half a pound, depending on the size of your processor). Pulse in short, one- to two-second bursts until the desired consistency is achieved, usually ten to fifteen pulses.

It's important to pulse rather than let the processor run. Pulsing tends to distribute the venison and fat pieces for more even chopping and avoids excess heat from friction that could turn your ground venison into mush.

The amount of fat you add (from the deer or beef or pork fat) is up to you, but for the best results, I recommend at least ten percent fat-to-meat ratio. Keep in mind that fat is where the flavor is and that it also adds moisture for a juicer end result.

If you are adding herbs or spices for one of my recipes, you can add them before you begin chopping.

Now that you have your deer burger "burgerized," it is time to wrap and freeze it. I recommend double-wrapping in one-pound packages using freezer paper. Follow the wrapping paper manufacturer's recommendations. Immediately freeze your deer burger, and make sure to date the packages. I do not recommend eating venison that has been stored more than twelve months in the freezer.

Now that you've read this and followed all instructions, recommendations, and helpful tips, you're ready to cook! So get to the freezer and grab a couple pounds of that deer burger, and let's go!

SOUPS
AND
STEWS

When it comes to the cold days and chilly nights of a Midwestern winter, I can't think of a more enjoyable experience than sniffing the aroma of a good soup or stew cooking in a Dutch oven.

Many hunters look forward to coming home or back to deer camp and sitting around a wood-burning stove with a pot of deer burger chili simmering on top. You can taste the love and pride in each spoonful of a good bowl of soup.

I have put together some of my favorite soup and stew recipes here. Although you may find several types of soups with similar names such as "chili," please read and try each one, because each will have its own flavor and each is truly delicious. Speaking of chili, I dedicated a whole chapter to all my favorite chili recipes for your enjoyment!

Remember, soup should be as much fun to make as it is to eat, so try them all with friends and family. Soup is also a great way to get buck master J. R. involved with cooking his venison harvest.

Uncle Buck Burger Soup

1 pound deer burger
2 small chopped white onions
48 ounces tomato juice
1 cup water
1 can cream of mushroom soup
1 1/2 teaspoons basil
1/4 teaspoon dill weed
1/4 teaspoon Italian seasoning
1 1/2 teaspoons marjoram
1/4 teaspoon oregano
2 bay leaves
10 ounces frozen peas
8 ounces dry noodles
Salt and pepper to taste

Sauté the ground venison with onions. Add the tomato juice and water. Stir well and simmer on low for about 5 minutes. Add the cream of mushroom soup and seasonings. Bring to a boil.

Add the peas and noodles. Simmer on low heat for about 30 minutes or until the noodles are tender.

Yankee Venison Stew

4 pounds deer burger
1 cup diced onion
14 diced potatoes
5 diced carrots
1 cup chopped celery
1/2 cup barley
9 cups water
2 tablespoons salt
3 tablespoons garlic powder
1 tablespoon black pepper
1 tablespoon dry parsley
1 tablespoon beef bouillon
1 cup brown gravy
2 bay leaves

In a large pot or Dutch oven, brown the venison and drain the fat. Add the venison back to the pot and add all remaining ingredients. Cook on medium heat until the vegetables are tender.

Great with buttermilk biscuits!

Colorado Dump Soup

1 pound deer burger
4 beef bouillon cubes
10 ounces tomato sauce
3 quarts water
$^1/_2$ teaspoon garlic salt
1 teaspoon ground black pepper
1 large chopped yellow onion
1 tablespoon basil
1 tablespoon parsley flakes
1 10-ounce can mushrooms, chopped
3 10-ounce cans mixed vegetables
$^1/_2$ pound egg noodles
1 10-ounce can tomatoes, chopped

Dump the water in a large cooking pot and bring to a boil. Add the bouillon cubes, tomato sauce, garlic salt, pepper, parsley, onion, and basil.

Place the venison in a medium-size cooking pot, and cook on medium heat until no longer pink. Drain the fat, and add the cooked venison into the large pot. Simmer for about 10 minutes on medium heat.

Add the vegetables, mushrooms, tomatoes, and noodles. Cook the soup on medium heat until the noodles are tender.

Deer Camp Chowder

1 pound deer burger
14 ounces diced tomatoes
1 small chopped white onion
3 sliced potatoes
3 tablespoons flour
2 tablespoons chili powder
3 minced garlic cloves
1 chopped green bell pepper
Salt and pepper to taste

Sauté the deer burger in a large pressure cooker. Add the tomatoes, onion, potatoes, garlic, green bell pepper, salt, and pepper.

Mix thoroughly. Cover securely and cook on high until steam is created. Place a weight on the cover stem.

When the weight begins to rock, turn the heat down to medium to allow the weight to rock gently and cook for about 10 minutes.

Cool the pot by passing cold water over the cover, and remove the weight carefully. Open the cover carefully after the steam has been totally vented.

Make a paste from the chili powder and flour, and add to pressure cooker. Heat on medium, uncovered, and serve hot.

10-Pointer Spicy Venison Potato Soup

$^1/_2$ **pound deer burger**
$^1/_2$ **cup chopped yellow onion**
$^1/_2$ **cup chopped celery**
1 16-ounce can chopped tomatoes
2 cups potatoes, peeled and diced
1 cup beef broth
2 cups water
1 tablespoon chili powder
$^1/_2$ **teaspoon garlic salt**
1 tablespoon Worcestershire sauce
1 cup cooked peas

Brown the venison burger in a large saucepan, and drain the fat. Add the onion and celery. Cook until the veggies are tender and crisp. Stir in the tomatoes, potatoes, broth, water, chili powder, salt, and Worchestershire sauce. Cover and cook until the potatoes are tender. Stir in the peas, and simmer for about 5 more minutes. Serve hot.

Timber Vittles (Venison Goulash)

1 pound deer burger
10 ounces stewed tomatoes
10 ounces tomato sauce
1 16- to 20-ounce package pasta shells
1 cup green onions
10 ounces drained mushrooms
1 chopped green pepper
$^1/_2$ **tablespoon garlic salt**
Black pepper to taste

In a large pot, brown the deer burger with onions. Drain. Add the tomatoes and tomato sauce. Simmer for about 20 minutes on low heat.

While meat is simmering, cook the macaroni according to the package directions. Drain and add the macaroni and remaining ingredients to pot. Simmer for another 15 minutes and serve hot. You can add vegetable juice if dry.

Deer Stock Soup

2 large deer bones, cracked
2 pounds lean deer burger
1 chopped white onion
3 cups long rice
$^1/_4$ teaspoon nutmeg
12 crushed peppercorns
$^1/_2$ tablespoon smoked salt
7 cups water
1 cup lager beer

Crack the bones after removing meat. Place in a large pot with the water and beer. Add seasonings. Bring to a boil, and then cover and simmer on low heat for about 3 hours. While stock is simmering, brown the venison and onions in a large skillet and drain the fat.

Strain stock through a tea strainer and then through a cloth to remove any particles. Add the stock, cooked venison, and onions to stock pot. Add the rice and remaining ingredients. Simmer until the rice is tender, adding more rice and liquid if needed. Salt and pepper to taste and serve hot.

Smokey Mountain Venison and Barley Soup

1 pound lean deer burger
1 cup diced celery
1 cup diced carrots
1 cup sliced cabbage
1 diced red onion
4 cups beef broth
1 1/2 cups diced canned tomatoes
1/3 cup uncooked barley
1 teaspoon dried thyme
1/2 teaspoon basil
1/3 cup chopped garlic
1 1/2 teaspoons brown sugar
1 1/2 teaspoons balsamic vinegar
1 teaspoon Worcestershire sauce
Salt and pepper to taste

In a large saucepan, brown the venison and drain off any fat. Add the celery, carrots, cabbage, onion, beef broth, tomatoes (with juice), barley, thyme, basil, and garlic. Cover, bring to a boil, and then reduce the heat and simmer for about 45 minutes, or until the veggies and barley are tender. Remove from heat, stir in the brown sugar, vinegar, Worcestershire sauce, salt, and pepper. Check for seasoning, and serve with homemade crusty bread.

Whiskey River Cheeseburger Venison Chowder

I shot whiskey (for you, not the recipe)
I pound deer burger
2 potatoes, peeled and cubed
$^1/_2$ cup chopped yellow onion
$^1/_2$ cup chopped celery
2 tablespoons beef base
$^1/_2$ teaspoon salt
I$^1/_2$ cups water
2$^1/_2$ cups milk
3 tablespoons flour
I cup shredded cheddar cheese

In a large saucepan, brown the venison and drain. Stir in the veggies, base, salt, and 1$^1/_2$ cups water.

Cover and cook for about 15 minutes or until the veggies are tender. Blend $^1/_2$ cup milk with the flour and add this to the saucepan along with the remaining milk.

Cook, stirring until the mixture gets thick and bubbly. Add the cheese, and simmer until melted. Serve very hot.

Wild Bill's Deer Burger Soup

I pound deer burger
I chopped onion
I quart chopped tomatoes
3 cups diced potatoes
I cup dark beer
2 cups water
5 beef bouillon cubes
I cup sliced carrots
$^1/_4$ head chopped red cabbage
Garlic salt, to taste
Black pepper, to taste

In a large pot or Dutch oven, brown the deer burger and onions together until the venison is cooked and onions are tender. Drain off fat. Add the tomatoes with juice, potatoes, beer, water, bouillon cubes, carrots, and cabbage.

Simmer on low heat until the potatoes are tender, and season with garlic salt and black pepper.

Saddlebags Savory Venison Soup

2 sliced carrots

4 tablespoons chopped onion

2 tablespoons water

I pound deer burger

2 cups tomato sauce

I cup water

4 tablespoons dry red wine

I teaspoon sugar

$^{1}/_{2}$ teaspoon salt

$^{1}/_{4}$ teaspoon garlic powder

$^{1}/_{4}$ teaspoon ground black pepper

4 tablespoons shredded cheddar cheese

In a 1-quart casserole microwavable dish, cook the carrots and onions with 2 tablespoons of water, covered, on 100 percent power for 2 minutes.

Stir the ground venison into the partially cooked veggies. Microwave, uncovered, on 100 percent power for about 3 minutes, stirring once to break up the meat. Drain off the fat. Stir in the tomato sauce, 1 cup water, dry red wine, sugar, salt, garlic powder, and pepper. Microwave, uncovered, on 100 percent power for about 5 minutes, or until the mixture is heated through and the veggies are done.

Sprinkle with the shredded cheddar cheese, and serve piping hot!

Deer in the Cabbage Soup!

1 pound deer burger
$^1/_2$ teaspoon garlic salt
$^1/_4$ teaspoon garlic powder
$^1/_4$ teaspoon pepper
2 chopped celery stalks
16 ounces drained kidney beans
$^1/_2$ head chopped cabbage
28 ounces canned tomatoes
2 cups water
4 beef bouillon cubes
Chopped parsley

In a large Dutch oven, brown the deer burger. Add the garlic salt, garlic powder, pepper, celery stalks, kidney beans, cabbage, tomatoes, water, and bouillon cubes. Bring the soup to a boil, reduce heat, and simmer, covered, for about 1 hour.

Garnish with parsley, and serve hot.

DEER CAMP OUTDOOR KITCHEN CHECKLIST

If your camp is like mine, then you have a mess area. Be it a chuck wagon, mess tent, or chow pit, the outdoor kitchen is the headquarters of deer camp. I have put together a checklist for your outdoor kitchen needs. You can use this list even if you're a big-time hunter with an indoor kitchen!

After all, ain't nothin' meaner than a tired old hungry deer hunter!

☐ Large water jug and water bucket
☐ Coolers/ice
☐ Thermos
☐ Stove with fuel/propane
☐ Matches/lighter
☐ Charcoal/firewood
☐ Dutch oven
☐ BBQ grill/fire rack
☐ Fire starters/paper
☐ Tablecloth/tacks
☐ Plates and bowls (paper)
☐ Cups/mugs (paper)
☐ Plastic silverware
☐ Measuring cups
☐ Heavy aluminum foil
☐ Paper towels
☐ Trash bags
☐ Dish soap
☐ Clothes pins
☐ Cooking oil/spray
☐ Food containers
☐ Tarp for shade
☐ Bug repellent
☐ Camp chairs
☐ Saw/axe
☐ Clothesline
☐ Fire extinguisher
☐ Potholders/oven mitts
☐ Pots and frying pans
☐ Cooking utensils
☐ Tongs
☐ Skewers/grill forks
☐ Can/bottle opener
☐ Pie irons
☐ Folding table
☐ Mixing bowl
☐ Cutting board
☐ Zip-top bags
☐ Napkins
☐ Dish pan
☐ Dish rags/towels
☐ Scrub pads
☐ Seasonings
☐ Potato peeler
☐ Dust brush
☐ Poles/rope/stakes
☐ First aid kit
☐ Plastic grocery bags
☐ Work gloves
☐ Dinner bell

Bayou Billy's Venison Cheesy Soup

1 pound deer burger
1 diced onion
1 minced garlic clove
2 cups Italian-style diced tomatoes
7 cups water
5 beef bouillon cubes
3 chopped carrots
4 cubed potatoes
1 cup corn
1 cup green beans
3 chopped celery ribs
1 cup ditalini pasta shells
8 ounces cubed Velveeta cheese
1 cup milk
3 tablespoons flour

In a 5-quart stock pot, brown the ground venison with the onion and garlic.

Add the tomatoes, water, bouillon, carrots, potatoes, corn, green beans, and celery. Simmer about 15 minutes until the veggies are tender. Add the uncooked pasta, and continue to simmer for about 10 minutes. Add the cubed Velveeta, and stir in until melted. In a small mixing bowl, combine the milk and flour, and whisk until smooth. Add the mixture to the simmering soup, and stir until the soup thickens. Serve hot.

Buck-in-Rut Soup

1 pound deer burger
1 cup chopped green onions
1 cup diced potatoes
1 cup sliced carrots
32 ounces canned tomatoes
1 cup sliced celery
$1/4$ cup quick rice, uncooked
2 cups water
1 cup beer
12 cans ice-cold beer (for you, not the recipe)
4 teaspoons salt
$1/4$ teaspoon basil
$1/4$ teaspoon thyme
1 bay leaf

In a large pot or Dutch oven, brown the ground venison and onions, and drain the fat. Add the rest of the ingredients. Bring soup to a boil, cover, and simmer for about an hour.

Sibs Doeball Soup

2 quarts water
25 small venison meatballs
16 ounces tomato sauce
2 bouillon cubes
$^1/_2$ teaspoon dried oregano
$^1/_2$ teaspoon dried basil
$^1/_4$ teaspoon dried thyme
$^1/_4$ teaspoon garlic salt
$^1/_4$ teaspoon ground black pepper
3 sliced celery stalks
2 minced garlic cloves
1 cup elbow macaroni, uncooked
Parmesan cheese

Bring the water to a boil in a large saucepan. Add the venison meatballs, tomato sauce, bouillon, oregano, basil, thyme, garlic salt, pepper, celery, carrots, and garlic. Simmer for about 30 minutes. Add the macaroni, and cook until pasta is tender. Top with the Parmesan cheese, and serve hot.

Hunting Lodge Stew

This is without a doubt my most requested recipe using ground venison.

3 pounds deer burger
4 tablespoons olive oil
1 chopped onion
1 chopped carrot
3 cups red wine
1 cup beef stock
$1/2$ cup sun-dried tomatoes
16 ounces frozen artichoke hearts
1 tablespoon arrowroot
6 tablespoons butter
1 tablespoon grated lemon rind
1 chopped garlic clove
$1/2$ teaspoon salt
$1/2$ teaspoon white pepper
Parsley

Brown the ground venison, and remove from pan. Sauté the onion and carrot in the oil. Return the meat to the pan, and add the wine and stock. Bring to a boil and add the sun-dried tomatoes.

In another pan, boil the frozen artichoke hearts for about 20 minutes and then add to the stew. Cover the pot with foil, pressing down so there is no space between the foil and liquid. Put the lid on the pan, and simmer for about 25 minutes. When done, drain the juices into a frying pan and thicken with the arrowroot. Add the juices back to the meat. Whisk the butter in the meat, and add the lemon rind, garlic, salt, pepper, and parsley.

Poor Hunter's Soup

1 pound lean deer burger
6 potatoes, peeled and diced
4 cups whole milk
2 chopped white onions
3 cups uncooked macaroni
1 teaspoon garlic salt
1 teaspoon white pepper

In a large skillet, brown the venison, and drain off fat. Place the potatoes in a large pot, and boil for about 20 minutes. Pour out half the potato water.

Add the browned venison to the potatoes and remaining water, along with the milk, chopped onions, and uncooked macaroni. Simmer uncovered for about 15 minutes or until the macaroni is tender. Season to taste with garlic salt and white pepper.

Fancy Pants Meatball Soup

This serves 1 person. Double for two!

2 tablespoons rice
1 cup water
2 ounces deer burger
1 beaten egg
1 tablespoon grated onion
$1/4$ teaspoon garlic
$1/4$ teaspoon parsley
$1/4$ teaspoon nutmeg
2 tablespoons dry red wine
$1 1/4$ cups beef stock
Salt and pepper to taste

Add the rice to 1 cup of water. Boil for about 5 minutes; drain well. Blend the rice, ground venison, egg, onion, garlic, parsley, and nutmeg; form into small meatballs.

Add wine to stock; bring to a boil. Drop the meatballs into the hot broth, one at a time. Bring to a boil again; reduce the heat. Simmer for about 20 minutes. Add salt and pepper.

Cousin Rick's Deer Dung Soup

2 pounds deer burger
1 slice wheat bread
1/2 cup dark beer
1 egg
2 teaspoons fresh parsley
1/2 cup grated Parmesan cheese
1/2 teaspoon salt
1/4 teaspoon freshly ground black pepper
14 ounces chicken stock
14 ounces Italian-style diced tomatoes
3/4 cup Italian-cut green beans
3/4 cup pasta shells

Heat oven to 425 degrees. Moisten bread with beer, and squeeze out any excess. Combine the beer-soaked bread with the venison, egg, parsley, Parmesan cheese, salt, and pepper. Mix these ingredients lightly but thoroughly, and shape into 1-inch balls. Place the balls in a shallow baking dish sprayed with cooking spray. Bake for about 20 minutes.

Meanwhile, in a large saucepan, combine stock, tomatoes, and green beans. Cover and bring to a boil. Stir in the pasta. Cover and simmer for about 5 minutes. Add the meatballs. Simmer uncovered for another 8 minutes or until the pasta shells are tender. Remove from heat, and let stand 4 minutes. Sprinkle with Parmesan cheese.

Hank's Onion Patch Soup

1/2 pound deer burger
1 tablespoon butter
10 finely sliced onions
10 ounces beef stock
1 cup water
3 beef bouillon cubes

In a large kettle, brown the butter and deer burger. Add the sliced onions, beef stock, water, and bouillon cubes. Simmer soup for about 45 minutes on low heat, and serve.

Fort Madison Pride Stew

4 cups water
1 1/2 cups dry couscous
2 tablespoons olive oil
1 pound deer burger
1 chopped onion
1 chopped green bell pepper
2 minced garlic cloves
1 cup marinated artichoke hearts with liquid
2 teaspoons capers with liquid
14 green olives
15 ounces chopped canned tomatoes, drained
2 tablespoons white wine
1 tablespoon orange juice
2 teaspoons sumac powder
1 teaspoon crushed red pepper
1 teaspoon dried basil
1 teaspoon cumin
1 teaspoon minced ginger root
1 teaspoon black pepper

In a medium saucepan, bring 3 cups of water to a boil, and stir in the couscous. Remove from heat, cover, and let sit for 5 minutes. Heat the olive oil in a skillet over medium heat, and sauté the venison, onion, and green pepper until the venison is browned and the green pepper is tender. Mix in the garlic, and continue to cook and stir for another 3 minutes. Mix in the artichoke hearts with liquid, capers with liquid, and olives. Stir in the tomatoes, wine, orange juice, and 1 cup water. Season with sumac powder, red pepper, basil, cumin, ginger, and black pepper.

Simmer on low heat for about 15 minutes.

Wild Side Jambalaya

1 cup cooked deer burger

1 cup diced ham

2 chopped onions

2 diced celery stalks

1 chopped green bell pepper

20 ounces canned stewed tomatoes, with juice

$1/4$ cup tomato paste

3 minced garlic cloves

1 tablespoon minced parsley

$1/2$ teaspoon thyme

2 whole cloves

2 tablespoons olive oil

1 cup long-grain rice

1 pound shrimp, peeled

In a large slow cooker, combine the venison burger, ham, onions, celery, green bell pepper, tomatoes, tomato paste, garlic, parsley, thyme, cloves, olive oil, and rice. Cover and cook on low for 8 hours.

Thirty minutes before serving, turn cooker to high setting, and stir in the shrimp. Cover and cook until the shrimp are pink and tender.

AFTER THE SHOT

You've done everything right. The buck is down. After you have made the fatal shot, it is a good idea to wait at least thirty minutes after the kill before searching for it. Deer will sometimes live a little longer even after a precise shot, and if you walk upon it while it is still alive, it will be spooked and the adrenaline will start pumping through its veins. When this happens, the deer will take off like a, well, a scared deer, and you will greatly reduce your chances of getting another shot or finding him.

One of the first things my father taught me as a young hunter was the importance of knowing how to follow a blood trail.

Knowing the types of blood color can determine whether or not it was the shot you intended. If the blood is dark red, the deer was hit in a vital area. If the blood is pink, this reflects a body shot and odds are it will be alive or has traveled a good distance from you.

When I bow hunt, I try to find a focal point of reference such as a rock, stick, or some type of landmark showing distance and where to start looking for blood after the shot. This saves time and also helps me find my arrow. Look for bedding area where the buck lay down while wounded. Look for heavy bleeding spots on the ground—it might be a good idea to wait a few more minutes before moving on. Of course if your luck is like mine, you shot him later in the afternoon and that means the sun will be going down soon.

I don't know if it's proven or not, but I have found that in most cases, a deer will head for water when wounded. When you find your downed deer, approach him with caution, in case he is wounded and just laying there scared. I always walk up on my downed deer ready to shoot if needed. Remember to give the deer a poke with your arrow or boot first before starting the chore of field dressing.

Most hunters like to take photos of their deer before field dressing and blood has soaked the fur. Always field dress your deer as soon as possible, and never drag it back to your truck or camp without field dressing first.

Remember, field dressing is one of the most critical procedures for ensuring great-tasting venison!

Hunt Woods Tater-and-Deer Soup

1 pound deer burger
18 small red potatoes
3 chopped leeks
3 tablespoons butter
6 cups chicken stock
2 cups milk
1 teaspoon white pepper
Garlic salt to taste

Place the potatoes into a large saucepan, and cover with water. Bring to a boil, and cook until tender. Meanwhile, brown the deer burger and leeks in butter. When the potatoes are done, skin them while they are still hot, and cut them into bite-sized pieces. Place the potatoes into stock pot with the chicken stock and venison/leek mixture. Season with garlic salt and white pepper. Cook over medium heat until simmering; then remove from heat, and stir in milk.

Buck Eve Stew

3 pounds deer burger
28 ounces stewed tomatoes, with juice
I cup chopped celery
3 sliced carrots
3 potatoes, cubed
3 chopped onions
3 tablespoons tapioca
2 cubes beef bouillon
$1/4$ teaspoon dried thyme
$1/4$ teaspoon dried rosemary
$1/4$ teaspoon dried marjoram
$1/4$ cup red wine
2 cups water
10-ounce package frozen peas, thawed

Preheat oven to 250 degrees. Brown the venison burger and drain fat. Place the cooked venison, tomatoes, celery, carrots, potatoes, onions, and tapioca into a large Dutch oven. Season with beef bouillon, thyme, rosemary, and marjoram, and stir in red wine and water. Place the lid on the Dutch oven. Bake for 5 hours. Add the peas during the last 30 minutes of cooking.

Crazy-Eyes Jenkin's Hunter's Bean Soup

I pound deer burger
$1/4$ cup olive oil
2 chopped carrots
I cup chopped white onions
5 chopped celery stalks
5 chopped tomatoes
3 potatoes, peeled and chopped
15 ounces canned kidney beans, drained
3 quarts chicken broth
I tablespoon cayenne pepper
$1/2$ cup tomato paste
I teaspoon smoked salt
I teaspoon black pepper

Place the deer burger in a large, deep skillet. Cook over medium heat until evenly brown. Drain the fat, crumble, and set aside. In a large stock pot over medium heat, heat oil and sauté carrots, onion, and celery. Add tomatoes, potatoes, kidney beans, and chicken broth. Bring to a boil, and stir in cayenne pepper and tomato paste. Reduce heat, and simmer for 25 minutes. Add the deer burger, and season with smoked salt and pepper.

McBrown's Irish Hunter's Venison Stew

3 pounds deer burger
6 chopped carrots
2 chopped onions
2 cups cubed potatoes
I tablespoon brown sugar
3 tablespoons tapioca flour
I cup vegetable juice

Preheat oven to 250 degrees. In a large skillet, brown venison, and drain the fat. In a large roasting pan, combine the cooked venison, carrots, onions, and potatoes. In a separate bowl, combine the sugar, tapioca flour, and juice, mixing well. Pour mixture over the meat and veggies, and cover tightly with foil. Bake in the oven for about 5 hours.

OH NUTS!

Cousin Rick took his son Travis hunting for the first time. Rick said, "Stay here and be very quiet. I'll be across the timber."

A few minutes later, Rick heard a bloodcurdling scream and ran back to his son. "What's wrong?" Rick asked. "I told you to be quiet."

Travis answered, "Look, dad, I was quiet when the snake slithered across my boot. I was quiet when the coyote breathed down my neck. I didn't move a muscle when the skunk climbed over my shoulder. I closed my eyes and held my breath when the wasp stung me. I didn't cough when I swallowed the gnat. I didn't cuss or scratch when the poison oak started itching. But when the two chipmunks crawled up my pant legs and said, 'Should we eat them here or take them with us?' Well, I guess I just panicked."

Triple K Ranch Venison Bread Soup

1 pound deer burger
6 potatoes, peeled and chopped
2 chopped onions
1 sliced carrot
1 sliced celery stalk
4 cubes chicken bouillon
1 tablespoon parsley
5 cups water
1 teaspoon garlic salt
1 teaspoon white pepper
1/3 cup butter
2 cups flour
1 egg
1 teaspoon salt
1 cup milk
12 ounces evaporated milk

In a large skillet, brown venison burger, drain off fat, and set aside. In a large stock pot, combine potatoes, onions, carrots, celery, chicken bouillon cubes, parsley, water, garlic salt, pepper, and butter. Simmer until the vegetables become tender. In a bowl, mix flour, egg, salt, and milk. Mix until dough is formed, and then roll into long strips. Cut the strips into small pieces. Add the dough pieces and cooked venison burger to the stock pot. Simmer for 30 minutes. Add evaporated milk, stir, and serve.

Keokuk Ridge Soup

2 pounds deer burger
4 10.75-ounce cans tomato soup
3 cups milk
2 cups water
8 potatoes, peeled and sliced
1 head cabbage, cored and sliced
4 sliced carrots
1 chopped onion

Heat a large Dutch oven over medium heat. Crumble in the ground venison. Cook, stirring often, until evenly browned. Drain excess fat. Stir in the tomato soup, milk, water, potatoes, cabbage, carrots, and onion. Bring soup to a boil, and then simmer over medium heat for about 30 minutes. Reduce heat to low, and cook for 1½ hours before serving. Salt and pepper to taste.

Timber Green Soup

4 tablespoons olive oil
I minced white onion
I minced garlic clove
6 potatoes, peeled and thinly sliced
2 quarts water
I pound deer burger
3 teaspoons salt
I teaspoon white pepper
I pound kale, rinsed and julienned

In a large saucepan over medium heat, cook onion and garlic in 3 tablespoons olive oil for 3 minutes. Stir in potatoes and cook, stirring constantly, 3 minutes or more. Pour in water, bring to a boil, and let boil gently for 25 minutes, or until the potatoes are very tender.

Meanwhile, in a large skillet over medium heat, cook the venison until brown, and drain off any fat.

Mash the potato mixture in a blender. Stir the venison, salt, and pepper into the soup, and return to medium heat. Cover, and simmer for about 5 minutes. Just before serving, stir in the kale, and simmer for 5 minutes, until the kale is tender. Stir in the remaining tablespoon of olive oil and serve.

Winter Stew

2 pounds deer burger
1 cup flour
1/4 cup butter
4 diced onions
2 cups water
1 tablespoon white wine vinegar
1 sprig thyme
2 bay leaves
1 teaspoon salt
1/2 teaspoon black pepper
12 ounces ale beer
1 slice bread
1 tablespoon mustard
2 chopped carrots
2 tablespoons brown sugar

Dredge the ground venison in the flour. In a Dutch oven, melt the butter over medium heat. Brown the venison in butter; then add the onions, and fry until glazed. Stir in the water and vinegar. Season with thyme, bay leaves, and salt and pepper to taste. Cover, and simmer for about 30 minutes.

Mix in the beer. Spread mustard over bread, then add the bread and carrots to the meat. Cover, and simmer for 30 minutes. Mix in the brown sugar, stir, and serve.

Deer Camp Opening Night's Campfire Soup

3 pounds deer burger
8 cups beer
2 egg yolks
1 cup sour cream
1 teaspoon cornstarch
1 teaspoon sugar
1 teaspoon salt
4 slices garlic toast, cut into 1-inch cubes
1 cup shredded Swiss cheese

Brown the venison, drain off fat, and set aside. In a medium kettle, bring the beer to a boil. Meanwhile, in a large bowl, beat together egg yolks, sour cream, cornstarch, sugar, and salt until well blended. Transfer the mixture to beer kettle. Add the cooked venison, and simmer while stirring for about 5 minutes.

To serve, divide bread cubes into four warmed soup bowls. Sprinkle cheese over bread. Pour hot soup over all right from the kettle.

Bleeding Guns Mabe's Deer Chowder

$^3/_4$ **cup diced onion**
$^3/_4$ **cup minced green bell pepper**
6 tablespoons fat
2 pounds deer burger
5 cups sliced potatoes
3$^1/_3$ cups water
I cup canned creamed corn
3 cups canned tomatoes
5 teaspoons flour
$^3/_4$ **teaspoon chili powder**
4$^1/_2$ teaspoons salt

Sauté onion and pepper in fat. Add the venison, and cook for 10 minutes. Cook sliced potatoes in 3 cups water until tender, and then add the sautéed onion, pepper, and meat with corn and tomatoes. Bring slowly to a boil. Stir in flour with $^1/_2$ cup of water. Add the chili powder and salt, and pour into venison mixture. Stir until thickened. Simmer for about 10 minutes, recheck for seasonings, and serve.

Farm King October Stew

2 pounds deer burger
1 pound thick bacon, cooked and diced
$^1/_2$ cup chopped yellow onion
1 cup **BBQ** sauce
1 cup lager beer
1 can stewed tomatoes
2 cups frozen corn
2 10-ounce cans potatoes, drained and cubed
1 teaspoon parsley
1 teaspoon minced garlic
1 teaspoon salt
1 teaspoon cayenne pepper

Brown the venison burger with onions and cooked bacon until the venison is no longer pink and the onions are tender; drain, and mix with BBQ sauce. Combine meat mixture with remaining ingredients in a slow cooker. Cover, and cook on low for 4 hours.

2

CHILIES

Cookin' chili with deer burger is a must for all out-doorsmen! Just like makin' jerky, all hunters have their favorite recipes that they cherish. Deer chili is without a doubt the number one soup made with deer burger. That said, I have dedicated a whole chapter to this wonderful soup.

I find it only fitting to share this letter sent to me by one of the readers of my monthly newspaper column. I do this out of respect to the deceased and as a lesson to all of my deer-hunting comrades!

Dear Rick,

It is important for men to remember that, as women grow older, it becomes harder for them to maintain the same quality of housekeeping as they did when they were younger.

When you notice this, try not to yell at them. Some are oversensitive, and there ain't anything worse than an oversensitive woman.

My name is Billy Ray. Let me relate how I handled the situation with my wife, Becky Sue. When I was laid off from my hunting guide job and took "early retirement" in April, it became necessary for Becky to get a full-time job, both for extra income and for the health benefits that we needed.

Shortly after she started working, I noticed she was beginning to show her age. I usually get home from fishing or hunting about the same time she gets home from work. Although she knows how hungry I am, she almost always says she has to rest for half an hour or so before she starts dinner. I don't yell at her. Instead, I tell her to take her time and just wake me when she gets dinner on the table.

She used to do the dishes as soon as we finished eating. But now, it's not unusual for them to sit on the table for several hours after dinner. I do what I can by diplomatically reminding her several times each evening that they won't clean themselves. I know she appreciates this, as it does seem to motivate her to get them done before she goes to bed.

And speaking of bed, that's where her age really shows. I go out and hunt all day, come home dead tired, and after a two-hour nap and a good meal, I'm ready, if you know what I mean. Age has gotten her so bad that she actually dozes off during my moment of rut! But that's okay. Her satisfaction in that area is important to a sensitive guy like me, and if she enjoys sleeping during our little trysts, what the hey . . .

Now that she has gotten older, she does seem to get tired much more quickly. Our washer and dryer are in the basement. Sometimes she says she just can't make another trip down those steps. I don't make a big issue of this; if she finishes up the laundry the next evening, I'm willing to overlook it. Not only that, but unless I need something ironed to wear to my Monday Pheasants Forever meeting, or to Wednesday's or Saturday's poker club, or to Tuesday's or Thursday's amateur night at the roadhouse, I'll tell her to wait until the next evening to do the ironing. This gives her a little more time to do some of those odds and ends like shampooing the dog, vacuuming out the boat, or cleaning out the garage.

Also, if I had a really good day in the field and it was wet and muddy, my guns are a mess, so I let her clean them—you know, get the grit off the scope and a little oil on the barrel. My hunting duffle bag is heavy, so I lift it out of the truck bed for her. Women are delicate, have weak wrists, and can't lift heavy stuff as well as men. But I did tell her I don't like to be wakened during my after-hunt nap, so rather than bother me, she can put them back in the truck when she's finished.

Another symptom of aging is complaining, I think. For example, she will say that it is difficult for her to find time to pay the monthly bills during her lunch hour. But boys, we take 'em for better or worse, so I just smile and offer encouragement. I tell her to stretch it out over two or even three days. That way she won't have to rush so much.

I also remind her that missing lunch completely now and then wouldn't hurt her any (if you know what I mean). I like to think that tactics is one of my strong points.

When doing simple jobs, she seems to think she needs more rest periods. She had to take a break when she was only half finished mowing the yard. I try not to make a scene. I'm a fair man. I tell her to fix herself a nice, big, cold glass of freshly squeezed lemonade and just sit for a while. And, as long as she is making one for herself, she may as well make one for me, too, and then take her break by my hammock. That way she can talk with me until I fall asleep.

I know that I probably look like a saint the way I support Becky. I'm not saying that showing this much consideration is easy. Many men will find it difficult. Some will find it impossible! Nobody knows better than I do how frustrating women get as they get older.

However, guys, even if you just use a little more tact and less criticism of your aging wife because of this letter, I will consider that writing it was well worthwhile. After all, we are put on this earth to help each other . . .

Yours truly,
Billy Ray

Editor's Note: Billy Ray died suddenly Thursday, June 5. His wife Becky was arrested, but the grand jury accepted her defense that he accidentally sat on his Remington 1100. She was released on Friday, June 6.

Feed Your Posse Chili

This recipe serves about 1200.

100 pounds pinto beans
50 large chopped onions
4 cups jalapeño chilies with juice
4 cups chili powder
3 cans light beer
Salt and pepper to taste
42 pounds deer burger

Soak the beans overnight. In a very large kettle, boil beans on high heat. Add the onions, jalapeños with juice, chili powder, beer, salt, and pepper.

In a very large pan, brown the venison, and drain the fat. Add the venison to kettle, and simmer on low heat for about 6 hours. Adjust thickness of soup with water.

Spunky Peterson's Deer Chili

1 pound deer burger
1 pound dried pinto beans
6-ounce can of tomato paste
2 cups chopped onions
3 tablespoons hot unspiced chili powder
1 tablespoon ground cumin
Salt
Water

Soak beans in water, covered, overnight. In a large Dutch oven, cook venison until browned, stirring to keep crumbly, and drain off fat. Add the tomato paste, onions, and drained beans. Mix the chili powder and cumin, and season to taste with salt. Stir into mixture.

Bring to a boil, reduce heat, cover, and simmer until beans are tender, about $5^{1}/_{2}$ hours.

Rick's Champion "92" Venison Chili

3 large white onions
2 green peppers
3 celery stalks
3 cloves garlic
2 jalapeño peppers
2 tablespoons olive oil
10 pounds deer burger
8 ounces diced green chilies
30 ounces stewed tomatoes
15 ounces tomato sauce
6 ounces tomato paste
8 ounces chili powder
2 tablespoons cumin
3 tablespoons Tabasco sauce
12 ounces ale beer
12 ounces mineral water
3 bay leaves
Garlic salt and pepper to taste

In a large Dutch oven or soup kettle, chop and sauté the onions, pepper, celery, garlic, and jalapeños in olive oil. Add the venison, and cook until venison is browned and veggies are tender. Add the remaining ingredients and just enough mineral water to cover the top of the mixture. Cook on low heat for about 4 hours, stirring about every 15 minutes.

Mississippi Deer Chili Soup

6 pounds deer burger
I cup corn oil
3 ounces chili powder
6 tablespoons cumin
2 tablespoons MSG
7 minced garlic cloves
3 chopped red onions
I cup lager beer or water
7 dried chili pods, boiled 30 minutes in beer
I ounce red pepper sauce
I tablespoon oregano
2 tablespoons paprika
2 tablespoons cider vinegar
3 cups beef stock
4 ounces diced green chilies
16 ounces stewed tomatoes
I tablespoon Tabasco sauce
2 tablespoons masa flour

In a large soup kettle or Dutch oven, brown the venison in corn oil, adding freshly ground black pepper to taste. Drain the fat from the meat, and add chili powder, cumin, MSG, garlic, and onions. Cook for about 45 minutes, adding as little water or beer as necessary. Stir every 5 minutes.

Remove the skins from the boiled chili pods. Mash the pulp, and add to meat mixture. Add the red pepper sauce, oregano, paprika, vinegar, $2/3$ of the beef stock, green chilies, stewed tomatoes, and Tabasco sauce. Simmer for about 50 minutes, stirring every 5 minutes.

Dissolve the masa flour into the remaining beef stock, and then pour into chili. Simmer another 30 minutes, stirring every 5 minutes.

Saint Louie Stagecoach Chili

5 minced onions
10 pounds deer burger
¹/₄ cup oil
2 minced garlic cloves
2 pounds ground sausage
7 ounces whole green chilies, minced
15 ounces tomato sauce
1 pound chopped cherry tomatoes
1 tablespoon cumin
1 teaspoon salt
1 teaspoon oregano
1 tablespoon dry mustard
1 ounce tequila
1 can Corona beer
3 ounces chili powder
3 beef bouillon cubes

In a large pot or kettle, brown onions and venison in oil. Stir in garlic, sausage, chilies, tomato sauce, tomatoes, cumin, salt, oregano, dry mustard, tequila, beer, chili powder, and bouillon cubes. Bring soup to a boil; then reduce the heat, and simmer for about 4 hours. Stir every 10 minutes. Do not stir for the last 30 minutes before serving.

COUSIN RICK'S TEN RULES ON HOW TO ACT AROUND HUNTERS OF THE OPPOSITE SEX

1. If he/she has seen game, and you haven't, think about it. He/she may know something you don't. Beginner's luck really doesn't help much during difficult conditions.
2. Don't let the smile fool you. If he/she has a plan for driving big bucks out of cover, he/she could do the brush-dogging just as easily as you but will use all his/her charms to make sure he/she will be the one in the best position to get the shot.
3. When it comes to skinning and butchering the deer, he/she does like a little help with sawing the pelvis and

lifting the quarters. Indiscriminate and ignorant advice will be ignored.

4. If he/she forgets some important item, like binoculars, or if you have a new pair to try out, he/she will be happy to wear yours.

5. He/she can, and will, field dress and drag his/her own deer, but if you just happen to be in the area, you can "show him/her how to do it."

6. If hunting is bad—really slow—he/she does not feel the need to leave camp unless the ambiance of the day demands. (A buck will probably come through camp when he/she's there anyway.)

7. He/she does not like to be ignored. If he/she has a buck hanging, get out your camera and your admiration. (Give him/her a chance to freshen up before taking the picture.)

8. If he/she's seeing game, and you're not, treat him/her like one of the boys; ask for help. If he/she tells you that you are hunting in the wrong area, listen.

9. If you've bagged a buck, and he/she hasn't seen any deer, offer advice, but never in a condescending way.

10. If this is his/her first time out, be patient and encouraging. Remember, this is hunting, not war.

Be kind and courteous. If you play it right, he/she may just share his/her homemade iced tea and deer jerky with you.

New Mexico Deer Camp Chili

$^1/_4$ **cup olive oil**
4 cups chopped yellow onions
3 pounds deer burger
2 pounds ground pork
$^1/_2$ **cup chili powder**
3 tablespoons cumin
3 tablespoons Mexican oregano
3 tablespoons unsweetened cocoa powder
2 tablespoons ground cinnamon
2 teaspoons cayenne pepper
4 cups vegetable juice
4 cups beef stock
8 minced garlic cloves
2 tablespoons cornmeal (use a thickener)
32 ounces dark red kidney beans, drained and rinsed

In a large skillet, over medium heat, warm the oil. Add onions and cook until tender, stirring often.

Meanwhile, in a Dutch oven, combine the venison and pork. Season with salt and pepper, and cook on medium heat until there is no pink left in the meat.

Scrape the cooked onions into the Dutch oven with cooked meats. Stir in chili powder, cumin, oregano, cocoa, cinnamon, and cayenne pepper. Cook, stirring every 5 minutes. Stir in vegetable juice and beef stock. Bring to a boil; then lower the heat, and simmer, uncovered, for about an hour. Taste and adjust soup for seasonings and simmer for another 30 minutes. Add the garlic, cornmeal, and beans. Simmer for another 10 minutes and serve.

Rumble Gut Chili

6 tablespoons olive oil

2 chopped yellow onions

4 minced garlic cloves

2 minced hot green chili peppers

3 pounds venison steaks, cut into small chunks

2 pounds deer burger

56 ounces stewed tomatoes

6 tablespoons red wine vinegar

6 tablespoons ground chili powder

4 tablespoons ground cumin

4 tablespoons Worcestershire sauce

I tablespoon cayenne pepper

2 chopped green bell peppers

20 ounces red kidney beans, drained

6 tablespoons fine cornmeal

Salt and pepper to taste

Heat the oil in a large Dutch oven or pot. Stir in the onions, garlic, and chili peppers. Sauté over medium heat until the onions are just tender. Add the cubed and ground venison, and continue cooking for about 8 minutes, or until the meat is no longer pink. Add all the remaining ingredients except the beans and cornmeal. Bring the soup to a boil; then reduce the heat to medium, and cook uncovered for about 30 minutes, stirring every 3 minutes.

Stir in the kidney beans and cornmeal. Taste and adjust for seasoning.

Deer in the Beer Chili

¹/₄ **pound dried kidney beans**
¹/₄ **pound dried white beans**
¹/₄ **pound dried pink beans**
¹/₄ **pound dried black beans**
¹/₄ **pound dried pinto beans**
¹/₄ **pound dried navy beans**
¹/₄ **pound dried red beans**
¹/₄ **pound dried cranberry beans**
I pound smoked bacon
6 chopped yellow onions
²/₃ **cup minced garlic**
¹/₂ **cup diced poblano chili peppers**
¹/₄ **cup ground coriander seeds, toasted**
¹/₄ **cup ground cinnamon**
¹/₄ **cup paprika**
¹/₂ **cup cayenne pepper**
I 10 ounces stewed tomatoes with juice
12 bottles Corona beer, I for the recipe and I I for you
5 pounds deer burger
Salt and pepper to taste

In a very large pot, cover and soak the beans together overnight, or at least 12 hours. Drain, and cover with fresh water. Cook and simmer for about 2 hours or until the beans are just tender.

While the beans are simmering, heat a large skillet. Chop the bacon, and cook until crisp. Add the onions, garlic, peppers, and remaining spices, and cook for another 6 minutes. Add the tomatoes, juice, and 1 bottle of the beer. Simmer for another 8 minutes or so.

In another large pan, cook the venison, drain the fat, and add it to the pot.

When the beans are fully cooked, drain them, reserving the liquid to add later if necessary, and add them to the pot. Simmer soup for about an hour on low heat, adding beer if soup becomes too dry.

El Blackies Taco Soup

1 pound deer burger
1 chopped onion
32 ounces canned whole tomatoes
16 ounces tomato sauce
15 ounces red kidney beans
15 ounces whole kernel corn
1 cup water
1 package taco seasoning
Sour cream
Chopped black olives
Grated cheddar cheese
1 package tortilla chips

In a large pot, brown the venison and onion. Add the remaining ingredients, making sure not to drain canned items. Use a big spoon to slightly mash the tomatoes before adding to the soup. Simmer on low heat for about 15 minutes.

Place the corn chips in the bottom of each bowl; pour the soup over the chips. Add a spoonful of sour cream, and sprinkle with cheddar cheese and chopped black olives.

"Deer Done Ate Our Beans" Chili

2 pounds deer burger
8 ounces tomato sauce
6 ounces tomato paste
16 ounces stewed tomatoes
2 tablespoons chili powder
1 teaspoon salt
1 teaspoon Louisiana hot sauce

Brown the venison in a large skillet; drain well. Combine with remaining ingredients in a slow cooker. Cover, and cook on low for 8 hours. Use warm beer if liquid is required.

Hartschuh's Ohio Hunters' "Chili"

4 whole allspice
5 whole cloves
I bay leaf
2 pounds deer burger
2 cups water
6 ounces tomato paste
I chopped onion
2 tablespoons chili powder
2 minced garlic gloves
I teaspoon sea salt
I teaspoon ground cinnamon
I teaspoon ground nutmeg
$^1/_2$ red pepper, cracked
2 teaspoons cocoa powder
3 teaspoons Worcestershire sauce
2 cups cooked kidney beans
6 cups hot, cooked thin spaghetti
Chopped green onions
Grated cheddar cheese

Combine the whole spices and bay leaf in a cheesecloth bag. Brown the venison; transfer to slow cooker. Add water, tomato paste, onion, chili powder, garlic, salt, cinnamon, nutmeg, red pepper, cocoa, Worcestershire sauce, and the cheesecloth bag with spices. Cover and cook on low for 8 hours, adding the drained beans for the last 40 minutes of cooking. Serve hot over cooked spaghetti, and top with chopped green onions and cheese.

Becky's "The Boys are Cleanin' Deer in the Garage" Meal

3 pounds deer burger
3 cans pinto beans, drained
2 cans enchilada sauce
3 cans tomato sauce
4 cups shredded American cheese
4 tablespoons minced onion
3 cups water
12 cups corn chips
1 1/2 cups sour cream
6 chopped jalapeño peppers

Brown deer burger; drain. Transfer to a large slow cooker. Stir in the beans, enchilada sauce, tomato sauce, 3 cups of cheese, onion, and water.

Reserve 3 cups of corn chips; crush the remaining chips and add to the slow cooker. Cover, and cook on low heat for 8 hours. To serve, top with sour cream, remaining cheese, and reserved corn chips. Place jalapeño peppers aside for the boys who have been in the suds before showing up to help butcher!

Hangover Heaven Chili-Cheese Soup

This chili soup was created in the fall of 1994 when six of us had too much fun at bow camp; the ingredients were what were left over in our cabin from the week before. This recipe is now served at least once during every hunt!

2 pounds deer burger
I cup chopped onion
I cup chopped celery
4 cups pinto beans with juice
3 cups diced potatoes
5 tablespoons onion soup mix
2 cups chopped carrots
I cup corn
I minced garlic clove
4 teaspoons chili powder
I cup warm beer
I shot bourbon
3 tablespoons hot sauce
2 large jars Cheez Whiz

Brown the venison and onion. Drain fat. Place in a slow cooker, and add all the remaining ingredients except the Cheez Whiz. Cover, and cook for about 4 hours on low heat, adding warm beer if needed. Before serving, add the Cheez Whiz. Serve hot!

Dark Woods Chili

4 tablespoons olive oil
1 chopped white onion
3 minced garlic cloves
1 minced green chili pepper
2 pounds cubed venison steak
1 pound deer burger
28 ounces canned crushed tomatoes
4 tablespoons red wine vinegar
4 tablespoons chili powder
2 tablespoons cumin
3 tablespoons Worcestershire sauce
1 teaspoon cayenne pepper
1 chopped green bell pepper
10 ounces canned red kidney beans, drained
3 tablespoons fine cornmeal, mixed with water to make a paste

In a large skillet, heat the oil, and cook the onion, garlic, and chili pepper until the onion is very tender. Add the cubed steak and ground venison, and cook until the meat is no longer red. Add all the remaining ingredients except the beans and cornmeal paste. Bring to a boil, and then simmer for about 40 minutes, stirring often with a wooden spoon. Stir in beans and cornmeal paste, and simmer for another 20 minutes. Salt and pepper to taste.

Thorn in My Side Chili

3 pounds lean deer burger

2 cups ice-cold water

4 cups beef stock

I cup dark beer

6 ounces canned tomato paste

8 ounces canned tomato sauce

6 ounces bitter chocolate

I teaspoon ground cloves

$^1/_2$ teaspoon cinnamon

I teaspoon vanilla

2 tablespoons brown sugar

I teaspoon ginger

I teaspoon cumin

2 tablespoons chili powder

5 tablespoons salt

2 tablespoons pepper

3 tablespoons Worcestershire sauce

I teaspoon garlic powder

3 bay leaves

I teaspoon onion powder

I teaspoon turmeric

I teaspoon ground coriander

I tablespoon lime juice

I tablespoon yellow mustard

I teaspoon oregano

Add the water and ground venison to a large cooking pot, and bring the mixture to a boil, stirring often. Add the remaining ingredients, and simmer for about 8 hours.

Niota Beer Chili

15 Mexican chilies, roasted, peeled, and stems removed
1 minced garlic clove
1 chopped white onion
1 pound deer burger
1 sliced tomato
1 teaspoon white pepper
1 teaspoon garlic salt
2 cups beer

Chop the chilies into very small pieces. Place the chilies, garlic, and onion in a large pan and cook until all is tender. Add all the remaining ingredients except beer, and cook until the meat is brown. Add the beer, and simmer on low heat for about 40 minutes.

Clapton's Stylin' Chili

3 pounds deer burger
3 cups cold water
3 cups cold beer
1 cup chopped white onions
1/4 cup minced garlic
12 ounces tomato paste
8 ounces tomato sauce
6 ounces chocolate
2 tablespoons minced cloves
1/2 teaspoon cinnamon
1 teaspoon allspice
1 teaspoon vanilla
1 tablespoon dark brown sugar
1/2 teaspoon ginger
1 teaspoon cumin
2 tablespoons dry yeast

Add the water, beer, and ground venison to a large cooking pot, and bring the mixture to a boil, stirring often. Add the remaining ingredients, and simmer for about 8 hours.

Old Uncle Ted, Try This Instead Chili

2 pounds lean deer burger
2 chopped white onions
1 minced garlic clove
2 tablespoons olive oil
Beer
1 teaspoon ground Mexican oregano
1 tablespoon flour
Beef stock to cover
1 teaspoon ground cumin
1 teaspoon ground coriander
6 New Mexican red chilies, seeds and stems removed
Salt and pepper to taste

In a large pot, brown the deer burger, onions, and garlic in the olive oil. Cover the mixture with beer, and bring to a boil. Chop the New Mexican red chilies, add to meat mixture, and cook until the peppers are tender. Add the remaining ingredients, and let chili simmer for 2 hours on low heat. Salt and pepper to taste.

Big Al's 30-30 Chili

3 pounds deer burger
2 tablespoons bacon drippings
6 cups boiling water
8 tablespoons rice
6 large dried red chili pods
Flour
Salt
Pepper
Minced onion

In a large Dutch oven, cook the venison in the drippings. When the deer burger is browned, add 3 cups of boiling water and rice. Cover and cook slowly until the rice is tender.

Remove the seeds and parts of veins from the chili pods. Cover the pods with the other 3 cups of boiling water and let stand until cool. Then squeeze pods in the hand until the water is thick and red. Add flour to chili water to thicken. Warm the red sauce in a small saucepan on very low heat. Place the red sauce on top of venison and rice, and season with salt, pepper, and minced onion.

Sammy's Little S.B.D. Chili Soup

I pound pork shoulder, cut into ¹/₂-inch cubes
2 pounds deer burger
3 chopped white onions
6 minced garlic cloves
I quart water
4 ancho chilies
6 dried red chilies
I tablespoon ground comino seeds
2 tablespoons Mexican oregano
Salt and pepper

Place the pork cubes and deer burger in a large Dutch oven, and cook until all is brown and no red is showing. Add the onions and garlic, and cook until they are tender and limp. Add the water and simmer slowly while preparing chilies.

Remove the stems and seeds from chilies, and chop very fine. Add the remaining ingredients to the soup, along with the chilies, and simmer on low heat for about 2 hours. Salt and pepper to taste.

Rusted-Out Floorboards Chili

1 tablespoon oregano

2 tablespoons paprika

2 tablespoons MSG

12 tablespoons chili powder

5 tablespoons cumin

5 tablespoons instant beef bouillon

30 ounces malt liquor

2 cups water

2 pounds cubed pork

6 pounds deer burger

5 chopped white onions

12 chopped garlic cloves

1 teaspoon mole poblano

1 teaspoon hot sauce

10 ounces tomato sauce

1 tablespoon masa harina flour

In a large pot, add the oregano, paprika, MSG, chili powder, cumin, beef bouillon, malt liquor, and water. Let simmer.

In a large skillet, brown the meat in 3-pound batches. Add the drained meat to the simmering spices. Continue until all the meat is cooked and added.

Sauté the chopped onions and garlic until they are tender and limp, and add to the soup mixture. Add the remaining ingredients and simmer on low heat for about 60 minutes. Salt and pepper to taste.

Ramaondo's Pride

2 pounds deer burger
1 diced green bell pepper
5 ounces green chilies, drained and diced
2 tablespoons chili powder
1 tablespoon garlic salt
16 ounces tomato sauce
6 ounces tomato paste
$^{1}/_{4}$ cup tequila
1 cup water
16 ounces canned kidney beans, undrained
8 ounces canned sweet corn, undrained

In a large heavy kettle, brown the meat until no longer red. Pour off drippings. Add the green pepper, green chilies, chili powder, garlic salt, tomato paste, tomato sauce, tequila, and water, stirring to mix well. Cook over low heat. Add the kidney beans and corn. Continue cooking for about 10 minutes. Salt and pepper to taste.

"Now Who Did That?" Chili

3 pounds deer burger
1 chopped jalapeño pepper
2 tablespoons paprika
1 tablespoon onion powder
2 teaspoons cayenne pepper
2 teaspoons beef bouillon
1 teaspoon chicken bouillon
10 ounces tomato sauce
4 teaspoons ground cumin
1 teaspoon garlic salt with parsley
1 teaspoon black pepper
2 teaspoons MSG
7 tablespoons chili powder

Briefly sear meat, and then add jalapeño pepper tied in cheesecloth sack, paprika, onion powder, cayenne pepper, bouillon, tomato sauce, and water to cover. Simmer, covered, for 2 hours.

Add the cumin, garlic salt with parsley, pepper, MSG, and chili powder. Cook for another hour on low heat. Remove the cheese-cloth sack, and serve.

Little Billy's First Time Out with the Boys Chili

2 pounds deer burger
2 cups pale ale beer
32 ounces tomato soup
20 ounces red kidney beans
3 teaspoons minced chili peppers
I teaspoon instant onion soup mix

In a large pan, brown the venison, drain the fat, and add the remaining ingredients. Simmer on low heat for about 40 minutes, stirring with a wooden spoon.

MY BUCK WAS SO BIG . . . TOP TEN LIST

Every year after a long day of hunting, my buddies and I spend the evening around the fire telling jokes and swapping hunting stories.

Three years ago we started to try and outdo each other with "My buck was so big" stories. I have put together the top ten lies, and who knows, maybe your hunting party can out-lie ours!

1. To fit the rack in my trailer, I had to move into a triple-wide.
2. Before I shot this buck, I noticed his hindquarters leaving the ground whenever he dropped his head to feed.
3. My taxidermist charged me by the pound.
4. When I first found this buck's rub, I thought someone had started a clear-cut.
5. The rack looks so lethal, I needed a permit to bring it home.
6. Whenever I show someone the photo of my deer and me, they want to know who the kid with the beard is.
7. Even though I was sitting in a tree stand, it was a level shot.
8. Rather than hang the mount on a wall, I have to display it in a reinforced floor console.

9. When I brought the deer home, the ceramic buck in my front yard ran away.
10. If I removed all the velvet from antlers this size, I could make seat covers for my truck.

3

VENISON CASSEROLES

When I was a young buck growing up, the words "We're having casserole for dinner" meant mom had made Tuna Surprise again. And that meant the dining room was as dead as an opossum with coyotes singing taps! I grew up not being a big fan of casseroles. Thank the deer gods I overcame this childhood aversion, and now venison casseroles are one of the meals I enjoy most at deer camp!

Why not? Casseroles allow us venison cooks a chance to experiment with a variety of tastes and textures as we whip up a complete meal in one dish. They are easy to make, bake, and take! You can use all the leftovers in the fridge, like mashed potatoes. Cooked rice, roasted potatoes, and cooked pasta make great building blocks. Even a small bowl of leftover corn, peas, or carrots goes great in most venison casseroles.

Here are some of my deer camp casserole favorites for you to get started with. Don't be afraid to play around with the seasonings. (If you're like me you will anyway.) When you master these recipes, you can make them ahead and freeze them for up to two months before serving. If Momma would have used venison instead of tuna, I'd never have left home.

Venison Cobbler

1 diced yellow onion
$1/2$ minced garlic clove
1 tablespoon oil
1 pound deer burger
1 teaspoon smoked salt
$1/4$ teaspoon black pepper
$1/4$ teaspoon marjoram
$1/4$ pound sliced cheddar cheese
10 ounces canned tomatoes, drained
2 tablespoons Worcestershire sauce
2 tablespoons ketchup
1 package yellow corn muffin mix

In a large skillet, sauté the onion and garlic in oil. Add the ground venison and seasonings, and cook until the venison is browned. Spread the venison mixture into a baking dish. Arrange the cheese on top of the venison. Top with the tomatoes mixed with Worcestershire sauce and ketchup. Mix the corn muffin mix according to the package directions, and pour over the venison meat mixture.

Bake in a preheated 400-degree oven for about 25 minutes, or until the muffin mix is done.

Fat Rusty's Casserole

2 pounds deer burger
1 cup sliced onions
1 cup sliced carrots
1 cup chopped celery
1 cup sliced potatoes
Garlic salt
White pepper
1 quart whole tomatoes

Brown the venison and onions in a large skillet, and drain the fat. In a large casserole dish, place the browned venison and onions on the bottom.

Layer the carrots, celery, and potatoes on top of the venison. Season with the garlic salt and pepper. Pour the tomatoes over the mixture and bake at 350 degrees for about an hour, or until the potatoes are tender.

Venison Zucchini Casserole

1 pound deer burger
1 chopped white onion
1 tablespoon oil
1 cup instant rice
$^1/_2$ teaspoon oregano
$^1/_2$ teaspoon salt
$^1/_4$ teaspoon pepper
4 cups sliced zucchini
2 cups cottage cheese
10-ounce can mushroom soup
1 cup sharp cheddar cheese, grated

In a large skillet or Dutch oven, brown the venison and onion in oil. Add the rice and seasonings, and stir for about 3 minutes. Pour off any remaining fat. Layer half of the zucchini, the browned venison, and cottage cheese in a casserole dish, and then top with the remaining zucchini.

Top with the mushroom soup and cheddar cheese. Bake in a preheated 350-degree oven for about 50 minutes, or until the zucchini is tender and the cheese is brown and bubbly.

Shaky Pistols Casserole

2 pounds deer burger
2 pressed garlic cloves
1 chopped onion
30 ounces tomato sauce
1 tablespoon dried basil
10-ounce package egg noodles
1 cup shredded cheddar cheese
8-ounce package cream cheese (room temperature)
$^1/_2$ cup sour cream
$^1/_2$ cup milk

In a large skillet, brown the venison, and drain off the fat. Stir in the garlic, onion, tomato sauce, and basil. Cover, and simmer for about 30 minutes, stirring every 5 minutes. In a large pot, cook the noodles according to the package directions. Spoon the venison meat into a large casserole dish, and top evenly with noodles. Sprinkle with cheddar cheese.

Whip the cream cheese, sour cream, and milk; pour over the noodles. Bake, covered, in a 350-degree oven for about 35 minutes. Serve hot.

Bedded Buck Pie

1 (8-roll package) refrigerated crescent rolls
1 pound deer burger
1 chopped yellow onion
14 ounces mushroom gravy
10 ounces frozen mixed vegetables, thawed
$^1/_2$ cup shredded cheddar cheese
1 large sliced beefy tomato
Garlic salt
Freshly ground black pepper

Preheat the oven to 350 degrees. Unroll the dough, and separate into triangles. Arrange them to cover the bottom of an ungreased pie pan. Press the dough together to form a pie crust, and bake for about 10 minutes.

While baking, brown the deer burger and onion in a large skillet; drain the excess fat. Stir in the veggies and gravy; cook until heated through. Pour this mixture into the pie crust. Sprinkle with cheese, and bake for about 15 minutes, or until the crust is golden brown and the cheese is bubbly. Place the tomato slices over the pie, and bake for about 4 minutes more.

Venison Rice

2 pounds deer burger
1 teaspoon olive oil
1 chopped onion
2 tablespoons minced garlic
$^1/_2$ teaspoon pepper
8 ounces sliced mushrooms
1 chopped green bell pepper
1 tablespoon Worcestershire sauce
16 ounces beef stock
10 ounces cream of mushroom soup
$2^1/_2$ cups instant rice
$^1/_2$ cup shredded cheddar cheese

Cook the venison and the onion in oil until the venison burger is browned and the onion is tender and soft. Add the garlic, pepper, mushrooms, green bell pepper, and Worcestershire sauce. Stir in the beef stock, mushroom soup, and rice. Cover the pan, and bring to a boil for about 5 minutes, or until the rice is tender. Place this mixture into a large casserole dish, and bake for 15 minutes in a 300-degree oven.

When the baking is done, season with salt and pepper to your liking, and then sprinkle with the cheese. Cover, and cook for another 2 minutes, or until the cheese is melted.

Serve this one to the boys immediately after cookin'!

Cooter's "Man, I Don't Like Cookin'" Casserole

2 pounds deer burger
1 sliced red onion
2 cups quick rice
20 ounces thick and zesty tomato sauce
20 ounces beer
Garlic salt
Black pepper

Brown the venison and red onion in a large pan and drain fat. Add the rice, tomato sauce, beer, and seasonings to taste. Place this mixture in a large casserole dish, and bake at 350 degrees for about 45 minutes. Add water if longer baking is needed for rice.

RICK'S HUNTING TIPS AND TRICKS

Yeah, buddy, not only are you lucky enough to have the best deer burger cookbook west of Dinkyville, but as a bonus, my huntin' buddies thought I should include a few of our certified, qualified, and bonded deer huntin' tips and tricks!

Not bad fer a bunch of huntin' hicks that can entertain ourselves for hours makin' whistle sounds with an empty slug shell.

To help find your deer stand in the timber when it's dark, put small pieces of reflector tape on your stand. A small flashlight is all you will need to find it in the early morning darkness.

To assist in finding arrows, try putting a small piece of reflective tape around the end of your arrows between the nock and the fletching. The tape will not affect the flight of your arrows but will help you to find your arrows in the dark. Just shine your flashlight around where you shot and the arrow will light up!

When aiming your gun or bow at a moving deer, use your grunt call. In most cases, the deer will stop just long enough for a shot. If you don't have a call with you, whistle.

Never smoke in your blind or stand. If you're a smoker, use the patch or nicotine gum. Deer can smell smoke faster than your mother-in-law can count your empty beer cans.

On opening day, pack your lunch and sit tight during the normal 10 A.M. to 1 P.M. hunter's lunch time. You will be amazed at how many deer are chased out by hunters walking back to their trucks during this time. Who knows? That wall-hanger might just run your way!

When choosing a place for your stand, look for rubs and scrapes along deer trails or in a broad area of land. Before hunting this stand, pour buck urine on the scrape and hunt it one to four days later using rattling racks and buck calls.

When deer are running past your deer stand, don't worry about putting the crosshairs of your scope on the deer. When deer are close and running, just fill the scope with the brown fur and pop a cap. I have found that if you concentrate on the crosshairs on this type of shot, you will often miss. The best setup is to have your scope high enough so that you can use both the scope and your sights.

After downing a deer, move in on it slowly and carefully, watching its eyes at all times. If the deer's eyes are open and glassy, the animal is most likely dead. Use caution if the eyes are closed. This could mean the deer is only stunned or wounded. Remember, a deer's hoofs are razor sharp.

When tracking deer in snow, always be aware that most deer tend to circle back to see what is following them. Big bucks do this also.

If party hunting and a deer drive are in the plans, bring a watch and cell phone. It's irritating when a hunting party member is late and has no way of letting the others know.

If you are still or tree-stand hunting, always double-check to make sure your cell phone is either on vibrate or turned off. Many a wall-hanging buck has trotted off to the sound of a cell phone coming from a stand.

I'll have more good tips, including a hunting checklist, in the pages ahead. Now let's get back to some more great cookin'!

Bad Boy Bake

1 package macaroni and cheese
1 pound deer burger
$^1/_2$ cup chopped celery
$^1/_2$ cup chopped green bell pepper
$^1/_2$ cup chopped sweet onion
12 ounces canned sweet corn, drained
10 ounces spicy tomato sauce
1 cup grated Parmesan cheese
Garlic salt
Black pepper

Prepare macaroni and cheese as directed on box. Brown the venison, celery, green pepper, and sweet onion. Drain off any remaining fats. Stir in the sweet corn, tomato sauce, and macaroni and cheese. Pour this mixture into a casserole dish, topped with grated Parmesan cheese. Salt and pepper to taste. Bake at 350 degrees for about 25 minutes, or until cheese is brown and bubbly.

The Lonesome Dove Platter

2 pounds deer burger
1 chopped onion
1 cup wild rice
1 can cream of mushroom soup, undiluted
1 can chicken noodle soup, undiluted
1 soup can dark beer
1 soup can water
$^1/_4$ teaspoon cocoa powder
$^1/_4$ teaspoon cayenne pepper

In a large skillet, brown venison with onion until the venison is browned and the onion is tender; drain. Place in a large casserole dish. Add all the remaining ingredients, and mix well.

Cover, and bake at 350 degrees for about $1^1/_2$ hours, stirring often.

Boys, I gotta tell ya, don't let the sissy cocoa powder scare ya, this dish is great when you're done draggin' out that wall-hangin' buck!

Gus Fuss

2 pounds deer burger
2 cans tomato soup, undiluted
2 teaspoons garlic salt
I teaspoon black pepper
2 cups cottage cheese
2 cups sour cream
12 green onions with tops, sliced
16 ounces egg noodles, cooked and drained
2 cups shredded cheddar cheese

In a large skillet, brown the venison and drain off any fat. Add the soup, garlic salt, and pepper; simmer for about 5 minutes. Remove from heat. In a large mixing bowl, combine cottage cheese, sour cream, green onions, and noodles. Then layer noodle mixture alternately with venison meat sauce in a greased casserole.

Cover, and bake at 350 degrees for 25 minutes. Sprinkle with cheese; return to the oven for about 10 minutes, or until cheese is brown and bubbly.

Venison Harvest

1 pound deer burger
1 cup chopped onion
30 ounces diced tomatoes
2 teaspoons Worcestershire sauce
$^1/_2$ teaspoon chili powder
2 teaspoons garlic salt
2 cups sliced potatoes
$^1/_3$ cup flour
2 cups frozen sweet corn
2 cups frozen butter beans
1 chopped green bell pepper
2 cups shredded cheddar cheese

Heat the oven to 350 degrees. Combine the venison, onions, tomatoes, Worcestershire sauce, chili powder, and garlic salt. Pat meat mixture into a layer in a large casserole. Layer potatoes, flour, corn, butter beans, and then green pepper. Cover, and bake for about an hour; sprinkle with cheese, and bake for another 30 minutes.

Shaena Marie Ranch Vittles

I pound deer burger
I teaspoon basil
I teaspoon paprika
^{1}/2 teaspoon pepper
I tablespoon salt
I can tomato rice soup
^{1}/2 soup can water
I tablespoon Worcestershire sauce
2 cups frozen white onions, thawed
4 sliced potatoes
I bay leaf

Brown the venison, and drain the fat. Add the basil, paprika, pepper, and salt. Mix soup, water, and Worcestershire sauce in a large casserole dish. Add onions, sliced potatoes, bay leaf, and venison; mix well. Cover casserole, and bake at 325 degrees for about 2 hours, or until tomato sauce has thickened and the potatoes are tender.

Travis's Deer Camp Breakfast

4 slices Texas toast bread
I pound cooked deer burger
2 cups shredded cheddar cheese
6 eggs, beaten
2 cups milk
I teaspoon dry mustard

Grease the bottom of a casserole dish. Tear the bread into small bite-sized pieces, and place at the bottom of the dish. Sprinkle cooked venison over bread. Sprinkle cheddar cheese over the venison. Mix the eggs, milk, and mustard together; pour over casserole. Bake at 350 degrees for about 40 minutes.

Mrs. Kitty's Long Branch Fixin's

2 cups frozen lima beans
I pound deer burger
I teaspoon salt
¹/₂ teaspoon white pepper
¹/₄ teaspoon nutmeg
I egg, slightly beaten
2 tablespoons olive oil
6 ounces tomato paste
¹/₂ teaspoon paprika
I cup sour cream

Cook the lima beans according to package directions; drain, and set aside. In a large mixing bowl, combine the deer burger, salt, pepper, nutmeg, and egg. Form venison mixture into 1-inch balls. Brown venison meatballs in skillet with olive oil. Add tomato paste to the lima beans, and stir in paprika and sour cream. Add the browned venison meatballs and stir. Pour mixture into a greased casserole dish, and bake at 350 degrees for about 30 minutes.

Huntin' Across the Border Dish

1 cup yellow cornmeal
1 cup water
^{1}/$_2$ teaspoon salt
6 slices heavy-smoked bacon
1 pound deer burger
1 teaspoon garlic salt
^{1}/$_4$ teaspoon white pepper
^{1}/$_4$ cup chopped parsley
1 cup chopped yellow onion
^{1}/$_2$ cup chopped celery
1 minced garlic clove
15 ounces diced tomatoes
2 cups shredded cheddar cheese

In a medium saucepan, mix together cornmeal, water, and salt. Cook over medium heat, stirring often, for about 7 minutes. Pour into a greased casserole, and chill.

In a large skillet, fry bacon until crisp; drain on paper towels, and then crumble. Set aside. Pour off fat from skillet; return 1 tablespoon of fat to the pan. Brown the venison with the garlic salt, white pepper, and parsley in the bacon fat; remove, and set aside. Drain off excess fat, leaving about 1 tablespoon. Sauté onion, celery, and garlic in pan until tender; add the tomatoes and cheese.

Remove chilled cornmeal mixture from the fridge. Turn pan upside down to remove cornmeal mixture in one piece. Cut into 16 small squares. Set aside eight for topping, and then place half of the remaining squares into the bottom of a greased casserole. Top with half of the browned venison and half of the sauce and crumbled bacon. Make another layer of cornmeal cubes and meat, and another layer of sauce and bacon. Arrange the saved eight cubes around the casserole dish. Bake at 350 degrees for about an hour.

"Better an Old Dog than a Dead Lion" Casserole

I pound deer burger
I can pork and beans
I cup **BBQ** sauce
2 tablespoons brown sugar
3 tablespoons minced onion
8 buttermilk biscuits, uncooked
I cup shredded cheddar cheese

In a Dutch oven, brown deer burger; drain off fat. Stir in the pork and beans, BBQ sauce, brown sugar, and minced onion; heat until bubbly. Pour mixture into a casserole dish. Cut the buttermilk biscuits in half and place cut side down, over the meat mixture. Sprinkle with cheese, and bake at 350 degrees for about 35 minutes, or until the biscuits are golden brown and the cheese is bubbly.

THAT'S MY BOY!

It was a clear, cold Iowa December morning, and all the conditions for deer hunting were perfect. Travis sat still and quiet in the tree stand, hoping to get his first buck. Just after daybreak, he could hear the crunching of the leaves as a large buck made its way down the run toward his stand. His heart started beating. Moments later, a monster 12-pointer at least 28 inches wide stood still broadside not more than twenty yards away. Travis slowly raised his shotgun, clicked off the safety, squeeze, *boom!* The buck dropped instantly in his tracks. Travis was so excited—he quickly hung the gun on the screw in the tree, scampered down the ladder, and ran over to where the buck lay.

Reaching for his gutting knife to begin field-dressing the deer, he realized that he must tag it first. Not wanting to get in trouble with the Fish Cops, he laid down his knife, pulled the tag from his holder, filled it out, and placed it to the buck's massive antlers.

He reached down, picked up his knife to resume field-dressing the deer, and then the buck did something totally unexpected—it jumped up, snorted, and then ran back up the trail over a ridge.

Travis stood there in amazement for a moment, glanced back up the tree at his shotgun hanging near his stand, looked at the knife in his hand, mumbled a couple of choice words "that he knew better," and tore out running after the wall-hanger.

Moments after the buck crossed over the ridge top, there was a blast from another hunter's gun. Travis thought to himself, "Oh no, not my buck." As he reached the ridge top and crossed over, he saw the big buck lying down on the trail ahead of him as a hunter cautiously approached the downed deer checking it for dead. Travis ran up to the guy, and out of breath he explained, "That's my buck, huff, huff, that's my buck."

"Like heck it is," said the other hunter. "I just shot this one."

"No, no, look, it's got my tag on his rack."

The other hunter looked down at the buck, and sure enough, there were tags attached to the antlers. The hunter looked back at Travis completely exhausted and out of breath, holding his gutting knife, and said, "Boy, if you're man enough to tag 'em first and then run 'em down, you can have the deer!"

Stick to a Hunter's Ribs Casserole

3 cups sliced potatoes
I sliced onion
I teaspoon salt
2 pounds deer burger
I cup soft breadcrumbs
8 ounces tomato sauce
2 tablespoons water
I teaspoon prepared mustard
2 teaspoons Greek seasoning salt
2 tablespoons minced onion
$^1/_2$ teaspoon white pepper

Put the potatoes and onion in a well-buttered casserole dish; sprinkle with salt. Mix the remaining ingredients; spread on vegetables. Bake, uncovered, at 350 degrees for about an hour.

Festus Beans with a Limp

I pound deer burger

I chopped onion

I can pork and beans

I can red kidney beans

I can pinto beans

I tablespoon prepared mustard

2 cups ketchup

$^3/_4$ cup brown sugar

$^1/_4$ cup white sugar

12 slices bacon, cooked crisp, crumbled

Brown the venison with chopped onions. Combine all ingredients, except the bacon, in a large casserole dish. Top with the crumbled bacon. Bake at 325 degrees for about 70 minutes.

She's Been with the Bucks Dish

$^1/_2$ cup fine dry breadcrumbs

I cup milk

2 pounds deer burger

2 teaspoons salt

I teaspoon black pepper

I chopped white onion

2 eggs

8 cups prepared mashed potatoes

I $^1/_2$ cups shredded cheddar cheese

I tablespoon paprika

Soak the breadcrumbs in milk. Mix venison, salt, pepper, onion, breadcrumb and milk mixture, and egg. Spread in a large greased casserole dish. Bake at 350 degrees for about 45 minutes. Top with mashed potatoes; sprinkle with cheese. Return to the oven for about 15 minutes longer. Sprinkle with the paprika, and serve.

Hungry Hunter's Choice

I pound deer burger
I chopped onion
5 ounces green chilies, drained
2 teaspoons chili powder
$^1/_2$ teaspoon cumin powder
$^1/_2$ teaspoon garlic powder
$^1/_2$ teaspoon salt
8 ounces tomato sauce
I can of 10 refrigerated buttermilk biscuits
2 cups Monterey Jack cheese
$^1/_2$ cup sour cream
I egg, lightly beaten

In a large skillet, brown the venison with onion; drain. Add the chilies, chili powder, cumin, garlic powder, salt, and tomato sauce. Simmer while preparing the biscuit mixture.

Separate biscuits, and then separate each biscuit into 2 layers. Press 10 biscuit layers over the bottom of an ungreased baking dish. Combine 1 cup cheese, sour cream, and egg. Remove meat mixture from heat, and then stir in sour cream mixture. Spoon the mixture over biscuit dough. Arrange remaining 10 biscuit layers over the top of the meat mixture, and then sprinkle with 1 cup of shredded cheese. Bake at 375 degrees for about 35 minutes, or until the biscuits are golden brown and the cheese is bubbly.

Chester's Munchies

2 pounds deer burger
I chopped onion
15 ounces spaghetti sauce with mushrooms
10 ounces cheddar cheese soup
8 ounces tomato sauce
6 ounces canned mushrooms
^{1}/2 teaspoon garlic powder
Salt and pepper to taste
2 cups shredded cheddar cheese
I 8-ounce package noodles, cooked and drained

In a large skillet, brown venison with chopped onion; drain well. Stir in the spaghetti sauce, soup, tomato sauce, mushrooms, garlic powder, salt, and pepper. Simmer for about 5 minutes. Combine venison mixture with the cooked noodles; pour into a large baking dish. Cover, and bake at 350 degrees for about 45 minutes. Uncover, sprinkle with the cheese, and bake for another 10 minutes, or until the cheese is melted and bubbly.

Deer Run Bake

I pound deer burger
^{1}/2 cup chopped onion
16 ounces chili with beans
2 teaspoons chili powder
10-ounce can of cream of chicken soup
3 cups yellow hominy, drained
3 tablespoons sliced ripe olives
^{1}/2 cup shredded cheddar cheese

Cook the venison and onion until the meat is well browned. Stir in the remaining ingredients, except the cheese. Spoon venison and hominy mixture into a large casserole dish. Cover, and bake at 325 degrees for about 35 minutes. Sprinkle cheese over the top, and continue baking, uncovered, for another 10 minutes.

Moser's Cabin Breakfast Casserole

We have this every year for breakfast during Iowa's spring turkey season.

12 slices of bacon
1 pound lean deer burger
2 cups onion/garlic croutons
2 cups unseasoned croutons
$1/4$ cup melted butter
2 cups grated cheddar cheese
2 cups milk
8 eggs
1 tablespoon prepared mustard

In a large skillet, fry bacon and venison until no pink is visible and bacon is crisp; drain on paper towels, and crumble. Spray a large casserole dish with oil. Place the croutons in casserole, and pour the butter over top. Sprinkle the grated cheese over all. Mix the milk, eggs, and mustard together, and pour over cheese. Sprinkle the bacon and venison meat mixture over all.

Bake at 325 degrees for about 45 minutes. Allow casserole to stand 15 minutes before serving. Great with Tabasco sauce!

DEER HUNTIN' HICKS, DOGS, HUNTING, AND ROAD KILL TEST

2 Points: You take your coon dog for a walk and you both use the same tree. (Double points: Dog & Hygiene = 4 total.)

2 Points: Your grandmother has "ammo" on her Christmas list. (Double points: Hunting & Family = 4 total.)

5 Points: You have forgotten which coat is sprayed in doe urine and have worn it to church.

5 Points: You've been involved in a custody fight over a hunting dog. (Double points: Hunting & Family = 10 total.)

5 Points: Your hunting dog cost more than the truck you drive him around in. (Double points: Hunting & Truck = 10 total.)

5 Points: You and your buddies sit on your garage roof at Christmastime hoping to fill your deer tags. (Triple points: Hunting, Entertainment, & Friends = 5 points per person.)

5 Points: You've never tried to hit a deer with your truck . . . on purpose! (Double points: Hunting & Truck = 10 total.) 10 Points: If you succeeded in hitting a deer with your truck . . . again on purpose. (Double points: Hunting & Truck = 20 total.)

20 Points: You have the local taxidermist on speed dial.

Skeeter Gibbs is top gun in this category with 102 points. Skeeter's Christmas rituals are legendary. Every year (after he gives both Grandmas ammo), Skeeter and his three buddies climb up on the roof with their shotguns and a case of Elcheapies beer in hopes of bagging Rudolf. This eventually led his wife, Betty Lou, to ask for a divorce. She sued Skeeter for custody of their two prize dogs. Now Skeeter hunts with his 1980 Dodge Ram truck . . . no gun . . . no dogs . . . just the truck. Betty Lou says, "Christmas was an annual nightmare. Those idiots shot out every light in the trailer park. But those three stuffed skunks in the bedroom . . . I couldn't sleep. Their presence permeated the house all year long."

Rick's Jalapeño Deer and Corn

This dish ain't intended for your mother-in-law!

I pound lean deer burger
$^1/_2$ cup minced onion
6 cups frozen corn
3 cups cream cheese
4 sliced jalapeño peppers
I teaspoon minced garlic
I teaspoon Frank's hot sauce
I teaspoon seasoning salt
$^1/_4$ teaspoon black pepper
I cup shredded cheddar cheese

In a large skillet, brown venison and minced onion; drain. In a large mixing bowl, stir all remaining ingredients, except cheddar cheese, with venison and onion mixture. Place in a casserole dish.

Bake uncovered in a 325 degree oven for about 50 minutes. Remove casserole, sprinkle cheddar cheese on top, and bake for another 15 minutes. Serve hot.

Well, boys, that's about all the fun any one hunter could have with casseroles! So, before we move on to the next chapter, on jerky and sausages, let's check out some Fun Deer Facts!

DID YOU KNOW?

In the early frontier days of our history, the skin of a male deer was worth a dollar, which is how we got to calling a dollar bill a buck.

Antlers start to grow on bucks in mid-April. While they are growing, the antlers are covered in soft velvet and are warm to the touch. By September, the bucks begin to rub their antlers against trees, shedding or rubbing off the velvet. Then the antlers are pointed, sharp, and cold to the touch. The antlers drop off in March, usually one at a time. Small critters like squirrels will eat the antlers (a source of nutrients) lying on the ground.

Does normally give birth to twins.

Fawns are usually born in May or June. They start to lose their spots in September and are then considered to be adult deer, ready to breed fawn of their own.

Deer shed their fur twice a year. In late August, they shed their reddish-brown coat and grow a heavy gray winter coat. In March and April, they shed the gray winter coat and grow a reddish-brown summer coat.

Talkin' to the old boys, they say 95 percent of the scrapes bucks make in an area will be used again the next year.

Those same old boys tell you to look for beaver ponds running east and west. Since deer tend to travel north and south, they will likely travel around one end or the other, increasing your odds of seeing deer there.

4

JERKY
AND
SAUSAGES

You can dog a man's truck. You can laugh at his gun. You can say his dog is stupid and lazy. But you can't say a dang thing bad about his jerky or sausage without a fight!

A man takes a little more time and pride when it comes to his jerky and sausage makin'. And, let's get one thing straight, when you make jerky, there's going to be a mess.

We all know that deer jerky has been around forever and was the number one food choice of the cowboys and outlaws of the old West. But just in case you don't know the history of sausage, your old cousin Rick is gonna tell ya.

Sausage is known to be the oldest and most enduring form of processed meat. In some respects, it may even be considered the world's very first "convenience food."

As long as man has been carnivorous, he has used the animal's intestinal tract for sausage casings.

During the last thousand years, sausage making has come into its own as a venerable and highly developed craft. The practitioners of this trade have fostered a rich tradition. Families have handed down their sausage-making recipes over the generations with each "wurst-macher" contributing his taste and heritage to the art. Today many deer hunters have sausage made for them by local butchers or they send their venison to a specialty smokehouse sausage maker.

Smoked venison summer sausage is a big hit among deer hunters and their families during the holiday season. Head off to the den, drink a beer or two, sample a few types of sausage and jerky, and talk about the year's hunt.

It doesn't get much better than that!

Onion Ground Venison Jerky

2-ounce package of dried onion soup mix
$^1/_4$ cup water
2 pounds deer burger
$^1/_4$ cup soy sauce
I tablespoon minced garlic
I teaspoon curing salt
I teaspoon liquid smoke

In a bowl, combine the onion soup mix and water. Let stand for 10 minutes. Add the remaining ingredients, including the venison, and mix well. Cover and refrigerate for 12 hours.

When done marinating in the refrigerator for 12 hours, remove and put through a jerky press, or shape the meat into 20-inch balls. Top it with a mesh sheet. Arrange the meat rounds on the mesh sheets. Dry at 145 degrees for about 8 hours. With some dehydrators, you may have to turn the jerky rounds to ensure equal drying. Be sure to blot any fat from the balls or jerky squares. When the jerky is done, let stand for 1 hour, and then cut thin slices from the jerky balls.

Deadwood Soft Jerky

10 pounds lean deer burger

$^2/_3$ cup curing sugar

1 teaspoon cardamom

1 teaspoon marjoram

1 tablespoon MSG

1 tablespoon cayenne pepper

2 tablespoons black pepper

4 tablespoons liquid smoke

2 tablespoons water

1 teaspoon garlic powder

Mix the spices thoroughly, and then add the spices a bit at a time while kneading the meat like a dough. Put the meat in the fridge for 8 hours to allow the spices to work through the meat.

After 8 hours, roll the meat out to a $^1/_8$-inch thickness between two pieces of wax paper. Remove the top paper and score the meat into strips and place them in the freezer for about an hour.

Remove the meat and break at the score marks. Place the jerky on wire racks in a 150-degree oven, leaving the door open about two inches.

Turn the jerky twice during the drying, and rotate the racks if the jerky is near the heating elements and begins to dry too fast. Dry for about 6 hours, or until the jerky reaches the tenderness you desire.

Lazy Jim Jerky Meat

2 pounds lean deer burger
2 tablespoon Worcestershire sauce
2 teaspoons curing salt
I tablespoon liquid smoke
I teaspoon cayenne
Freshly ground black pepper

In a large bowl, mix all ingredients together, cover, and refrigerate for 8 hours. Place the cured venison on wax paper and roll to $1/4$ inch thick. Cut into desired strips, and dry in a dehydrator for 6 hours, patting off all fats.

Don't be fooled by this one: Jimmy sells his jerky for 30 bucks a pound! City Slickers, gotta love 'em!

Conrad Wilke's Jerky Vittles

5 pounds lean deer burger
4 tablespoons salt
I teaspoon curing salt
2 teaspoons cayenne pepper
2 teaspoons crushed red peppers
2 teaspoons chili powder
2 teaspoons yellow mustard seed, ground fine
2 cups corn syrup
I tablespoon black ground pepper

In a large mixing bowl, add all the ingredients, and mix well. Cure seasoned meat overnight in the refrigerator. Spread jerky evenly on drying racks; dry at 170 degrees in smoker for about 12 hours or depending on your taste. You can also use your dehydrator or oven. *Keep in mind that Wilke is in his forties now and don't make his jerky in an oven. He's a smoker kind of man! I don't argue with him about this; he's almost as good at cookin' jerky as me . . . almost.*

Jim and Mae's Pulaski Pride

Do this one right! I've hunted on the Stoker farm goin' on fifteen years now and Mae isn't very big, but she can get ornery! When dealin' with Mae, better mind your manners.

5 pounds lean deer burger
5 tablespoons garlic salt
1 teaspoon curing salt
2 teaspoons liquid smoke
1 teaspoon onion powder
1 teaspoon ground coriander seed
1 teaspoon chili powder
2 teaspoons white pepper
1 teaspoon cayenne

Mix all the ingredients together, and cure in the refrigerator for 12 hours. Using wax paper and a rolling pin, roll jerky meat to desired thickness. Dry in 170-degree smoker or oven for 12 hours.

Ja-Makin'-Me-Crazy Jerky

This is one hot jerky! Not to be ate by sissies, "ya mon."

2 pounds lean deer burger
1 package Jamaican Jerk seasoning
2 tablespoons curing salt
1 cup corn syrup

In a large bowl, while drinking Red Strip, mix all the ingredients together, and refrigerate for 12 hours.

Roll meat with an Appleton Rum bottle to desired thickness. Place the venison in the oven, while wearing a parrot head cap, and dry at 140 degrees for 8 hours.

When finished drying, cool in the refrigerator for an hour before eating. When eating, jam out to Jimmie B. or Bobby M. *Do you know that the island of Jamaica don't got any deer? They all eat goats. Goats, I tell ya! I'm from Iowa, and I ain't seen so many goats as I do running around the mountains and roads in Jamaica.*

Rick's "I Ain't Got No Goat" Jerky

3 pounds lean deer burger
$1/4$ cup soy sauce
$1/4$ cup teriyaki sauce
4 tablespoons brown sugar
I minced garlic clove
I tablespoon hickory liquid smoke
2 teaspoons grated ginger
Coarse ground black pepper

Press the ground venison meat into flat strips about 5 inches long by 1 inch wide and $1/4$ inch thick. Place one layer of venison strips in a dish for marinating. Mix marinade ingredients together in a bowl. After well mixed, sprinkle marinade sauce over meat, soaking well. Turn the meat strips over, and sprinkle with sauce again. Place the meat in the fridge, and cool for 8 hours.

Place the cured meat strips in dehydrator, and dry for 6 to 8 hours.

SURVIVAL KIT CHECKLIST

Three years ago I was bow hunting with a buddy who got very sick when a thorn punctured his hand. The thorn wound became infected, and that's what made my buddy ill. This could have been avoided if one of us had planned better and brought along a first aid survival kit. With that in mind, here's a checklist for you and your hunting posse to use.

☐ Band-Aids
☐ Peroxide swabs
☐ Iodine swabs
☐ Triangular bandage
☐ Small bag with bouillon cubes
☐ 1 kit of water-purifying tablets
☐ Waterproof matches/lighter
☐ 10 feet of aluminum foil
☐ Salt
☐ Fire flint
☐ Small kit of fishing lures
☐ Assorted split shot sinkers
☐ Assorted hooks
☐ Duct tape
☐ 30 feet of fishing line
☐ Sharp pocket knife folded tightly

Even though we live in a world of cell phones and global navigating devices, I highly recommend you carry a good first aid/survival kit in every vehicle, boat, and quad runner. Keep your kit in a zip-top baggie, and check the kits yearly to replace any items that have been used or damaged.

South Carolina Jerky Meat

3 pounds deer burger
4 ounces duck sauce
4 ounces whiskey
2 ounces hot sauce
$^{1}/_{2}$ cup wine
8 tablespoons teriyaki sauce
4 tablespoons soy sauce
I finely minced habanero
I tablespoon onion powder
I teaspoon garlic powder
I teaspoon chili powder
I tablespoon course black pepper
I teaspoon garlic salt

In a large mixing bowl, combine all the ingredients together, cover, and cool in the refrigerator for 24 hours.

Using wax paper and a rolling pin, form jerky pieces about $^{1}/_{4}$ inch thick.

Bake jerky slices in the oven for 8 hours at 170 degrees, or until desired texture and taste.

Shimick Forest Garlic Jerky

3 pounds lean deer burger
$1/4$ cup Worcestershire sauce
$1/4$ cup soy sauce
I tablespoon tomato sauce
I tablespoon vinegar
I tablespoon sugar
2 tablespoons garlic powder
I tablespoon onion powder
2 tablespoons curing salt

In a large mixing bowl, combine all the ingredients together, and mix well. Cure the jerky mixture in a covered plastic bowl for 12 hours in the refrigerator.

Using the wax paper and rolling pin method, form jerky into bite-sized pieces.

Dehydrate jerky at 170 degrees for 6 to 8 hours.

Mud on My Boots Jerky

3 pounds lean deer burger
$1/4$ cup soy sauce
$1/4$ cup Worcestershire sauce
2 tablespoons Accent
2 teaspoons seasoned salt
I teaspoon garlic powder with parsley
2 teaspoons onion powder
I teaspoon black pepper
2 teaspoons quick salt

In a large mixing bowl, combine all the ingredients together and mix well. Cover, and place in the refrigerator overnight. Form $1/4$-inch-thick jerky ropes or rolls. Bake in a preheated 150-degree oven for about 6 hours, or until the jerky ropes reach your desired taste and texture.

Old Timer Jerky

5 pounds deer burger
I can beer
I tablespoon liquid smoke
2 tablespoons onion powder
I tablespoon black pepper
5 tablespoons salt
I tablespoon brown sugar
I tablespoon lemon pepper

Bring all the ingredients except venison to a boil in a large pot. Let the curing marinade cool, then add the venison, and make a well-mixed loaf. Wrap the loaf in a plastic trash bag or grocery bag and refrigerate for 12 hours.

Make 2-inch balls with cured jerky meat, and bake in a 140-degree oven for about 8 hours. Check center of jerky balls for pinkness before removing from oven.

Hopsing's Bonanza Jerky

3 pounds deer burger
$1/2$ cup light soy sauce
4 tablespoons honey
4 tablespoons dry sherry
I tablespoon garlic powder
I tablespoon ginger
I tablespoon crushed red pepper
I tablespoon sesame oil

In a large mixing bowl, combine all the ingredients, and mix well. Place the mixed venison in a covered plastic bowl, and cool in the fridge overnight.

Using the wax paper and rolling pin method, roll out $1/4$-inch-thick molded jerky pieces. Place in dehydrator, and dry cook for about 6 hours, or until jerky reaches desired texture and taste.

IOWA'S SMARTEST HUNTERS!

After a good day of deer hunting, Rick and Bubba were dragging their dead deer back to their truck. Another hunter approached, pulling his along, too. "Hey, I don't want to tell you how to do something, but I can tell you that it's much easier if you drag the deer in the other direction. Then the antlers won't dig into the ground."

After the third hunter moved on, the two decided to try out his advice. A little while later Rick said to Bubba, "You know, that guy was right. This is a lot easier!"

"Yeah," said Bubba, "but we're getting farther from the truck."

Terry Lee's Old Navy Deer Salami

5 pounds deer burger
5 teaspoons quick salt
3 teaspoons black pepper
1 teaspoon cayenne pepper
2 teaspoons garlic salt
1 teaspoon liquid smoke

In a large bowl, mix all the ingredients, and cover. Refrigerate for 2 days, remixing meat every 12 hours for a total of four mixes. On the third day, form salami meat into firm rolls, and place on a broiler pan. Bake for 5 hours at 175 degrees. Turn the salami rolls every hour until the salami reaches your desired texture.

Shaena and John's Parris Island Bologna

15 pounds lean deer burger
2/3 cup quick salt
8 teaspoons coarse black pepper
8 teaspoons garlic salt with parsley
10 teaspoons Accent
1 teaspoon cayenne pepper
1/2 cup brown sugar
2 teaspoons liquid smoke
1/2 quart vegetable oil

In a large mixing bowl, mix all the ingredients together except the liquid smoke and oil.

Cover the ingredients, and refrigerate for 24 hours. After the mixture cures for 24 hours, mix the oil and liquid smoke together, and incorporate it into the meat mixture, remixing all.

Roll mixture into bologna rolls, and wrap tightly with foil. Bake at 200 degrees for 5 hours. When done baking, dry off any fats, and wrap bologna in freezer paper. Freeze bologna until ready for you and your friends to enjoy. Thaw first for 2 hours or more.

Tom Cat Burgess Sperry Salami

5 pounds lean deer burger
5 teaspoons quick salt
3 teaspoons mustard seeds
3 teaspoons garlic salt
1 teaspoon hickory liquid smoke

Mix ingredients in a large bowl, and refrigerate, covered with lid or plastic wrap.

Remix daily for 5 days. On the sixth day, form into 2-pound rolls with each roll 2 inches in diameter. Place the rolls in a smoker at 120 degrees for 7 hours, turning every hour. Use hickory or cherry wood for great-tasting salami!

Skunk River Park Venison Summer Sausage

2 pounds deer burger
^{1}/2 cup water
2 teaspoons liquid smoke
^{1}/2 teaspoon garlic powder
I teaspoon minced garlic
^{1}/2 teaspoon mustard seed
I teaspoon black pepper
I tablespoon quick salt
2 teaspoons sugar
I teaspoon Accent

Mix all the ingredients very well. Roll in three rolls as firmly as possible. Place rolls on aluminum foil with the shiny side of foil next to the venison meat. Wrap with seam side up. Cool in the refrigerator for 2 days. Punch holes in the bottom of the rolls. Place on oven rack and bake at 325 degrees for 2 hours. Chill the sausage before serving.

Cousin Rick Black's Lee County Deer Huntin' Bratwurst

25 pounds deer burger
³/₄ cup nonfat dry milk
I cup garlic salt with parsley
I cup dark beer
2 gallons ice water
4 eggs
3 tablespoons sugar
8 tablespoons onion powder
6 tablespoons black pepper
2 tablespoons ground mace
2 tablespoons jalapeño powder
2 tablespoons ground ginger
I teaspoon cayenne pepper
I teaspoon fish sauce
4 tablespoons cumin

In a large bowl or pot, mix all the ingredients together very well. Run this mixture through a grinder using a ¹/₈-inch plate.

Mix for 8 minutes, and stuff into hog casings. Smoke the brats in the smoker until the internal temperature of the sausage reaches 155 degrees. Immediately place each brat in ice-cold water until the internal temperature is 90 degrees.

Rinse briefly with warm water to remove grease, and wipe each sausage down with a towel. Store bratwurst in a refrigerated cooler, wrapped, until ready to serve.

Note: This is an award-winning recipe of mine. I modified the original recipe from my grandpappy handed down to me through my dad. I won first place in several county fairs in Iowa with it. Until now, I have never shared this recipe with anyone, though the following has been offered: cash, free meat processing, hunting and fishing trips, a pontoon boat, two hunting dogs, a 1992 two-bedroom camper, a bottle of five-star whiskey (from my brother-in-law), a cherry 1988 Heritage Softail Harley, and a copy of *Bag 'Em and Tag 'Em* signed by Rick Black (evidently Darren didn't realize that was me?). Last but not least, my son said, "Dad, I love your brats, however, I would add chunks of sharp cheddar cheese." Me, being the proud dad that I am, I agree!

Whitetail County Venison Sausage

4 pounds deer burger

4 pounds ground pork

I pound ground pork fat

$^1/_2$ cup chopped onions

$^1/_2$ cup chopped celery

$^1/_2$ cup diced garlic

$^1/_2$ cup chopped red bell pepper

$^1/_2$ cup sliced green onions

$^1/_2$ cup chopped sage

I teaspoon garlic salt

I teaspoon coarse black pepper

I cup ice water

20 feet casing for stuffing

In a very large mixing pot, combine all the ingredients with the exception of the casing. Add the cup of ice water to the mixture, and mix well with your hands. Stuff the mixture into the casings, and smoke the sausage until the internal temperature reaches 155 degrees. Immediately place smoked sausages in ice water to cool. Wipe off any fats on casings, and store in the refrigerator.

Timmy Brown's "I Got Me a Deer with Horns" Summer Sausage

6 pounds deer burger
6 teaspoons pickling salt
3 teaspoons mustard seed
3 teaspoons ground black pepper
3 chopped garlic cloves
I teaspoon smoked salt

In a large mixing bowl or pot, mix all the ingredients together, and place in the refrigerator covered.

Once per day, remove bowl from the fridge and remix mix by hand for 3 days.

On the fourth day, form the meat into 5 rolls. Place on broiler pan and rack. Place on lower rack of oven, and bake for 8 hours at 170 degrees, turning occasionally. Keep finished sausage in the freezer, dated and wrapped.

Country Boy Bow Kill Tube Steak

15 pounds deer burger
3 tablespoons mustard seed
I tablespoon whole peppercorns
I cup beer
¹/₂ cup pickling salt
I tablespoon onion powder
I teaspoon garlic powder
I tablespoon ground black pepper
I teaspoon anise seed

In a large mixing bowl, mix all the ingredients together, and place in a covered container. Refrigerate for 3 days, remixing daily. On the fourth day, pack into casings made from 8- by 10-inch sections of sheeting, seamed to make a tube. Tie ends. Smoke in a large smoker for 6 hours.

Cousin Rick's Deer Sticks

6 pounds deer burger
6 tablespoons pickling salt
I teaspoon garlic powder
I teaspoon onion powder
3 tablespoons liquid smoke

Mix all the ingredients together. Form into 4 sticks, and place in refrigerator, uncovered, for 24 hours. Bake on wire rack, so the grease can drip down, for 1 hour at 325 degrees.

OH, I GET IT!

One day after a good bow hunt Cousin Rick was cruising along a back country road in his old pickup truck, hauling home his big 12-point buck. All of a sudden he drove into a huge mud hole right in the center of the road.

Hopelessly stuck, Rick walked down the old dirt road to find help. After walking for about an hour, he came upon an old man with a four-wheel drive with a big winch hanging on the front.

When Cousin Rick told the old man about his wall-hanging deer and truck stuck in the mud hole, the old-timer said, "I'll pull you out, but it will cost you that big buck you're hauling."

Now old Rick was in quite a bind and was forced to give the old man his buck.

After he was freed from the mud hole, Rick complained, "You know, taking a man's deer, let alone his once-in-a-lifetime buck, is just downright mean. I'm surprised you're not pulling people out of the mud full-time."

"Can't," replied the old cuss. "It takes me the better part of the day to haul water for the hole!"

Hawkeye Tailgating Sausage

4 pounds deer burger
2 pounds smoked ground bacon
$1/2$ cup brown sugar
2 teaspoons salt
1 teaspoon garlic powder
1 teaspoon onion powder
$1/2$ teaspoon coriander
2 teaspoons white pepper
$1/2$ teaspoon allspice
$1/4$ teaspoon cinnamon
$1/4$ teaspoon savory
$1/2$ teaspoon liquid smoke
$1/4$ teaspoon cumin

In a large mixing bowl, combine all the ingredients, and mix well using your hands. Shape into $1/4$-pound patties, wrap, and freeze. Fry using little oil when ready for your tailgating vittles!

Switch Creek Smoked Venison Links

16 pounds deer burger
3 pounds smoked ground bacon
3 teaspoons garlic powder
1 teaspoon sage
1 teaspoon Chinese 5 spice
1 teaspoon soy sauce
2 teaspoons cayenne pepper
2 tablespoons fennel
4 tablespoons crushed red pepper
10 tablespoons Allegro

In a large mixing bowl, combine all the ingredients together, and place covered in the refrigerator. Refrigerate for 24 hours, stirring mixture every 4 hours or so.

Link the meat into casings, and convection smoke for 3 hours at 250 degrees.

Scar Belly Bonne's Deer Hunter's Sausages

4 cups chopped yellow onions
I bay leaf
I cup chopped green pepper
I tablespoon chopped garlic
I tablespoon sage
2 tablespoons cayenne pepper
I tablespoon hickory liquid smoke
$^1/_2$ cup beer
3 cups cooked rice
3 pounds ground pork
3 pounds deer burger
8 whole peppercorns
I cup chopped parsley
$^1/_4$ cup chopped green onions
I tablespoon white pepper

In a large pot, cook the onion, bay leaf, green pepper, garlic, sage, cayenne, and liquid smoke with $^1/_2$ cup of beer until all veggies are very tender. Cook the rice according to package directions. In a large grinder, add all the cooked and uncooked ingredients. Remix ground ingredients by hand and place into casings. Smoke, grill, or fry sausages. If frying or grilling sausages, boil first for at least 10 minutes.

NOT THE COLDEST BEERS IN THE FRIDGE!

One fall day, Cousin Rick was walking into a sporting goods store when he ran into his hunting buddy, Darren, walking out of the store carrying a bag.

Cousin Rick: "Hey, Darren, what you got in that bag?"

Darren: "In this bag I got me deer grunts."

Cousin Rick: "Deer grunts! I sure would like me a new deer grunt. I bet you if I guess how many deer grunts you got in that thar bag, you'll give me one . . ."

Darren: "Shoot, Cousin Rick, if you guess how many deer grunts I got in this bag I'll give you both of them."

Cousin Rick: "Okay . . . five!"

5

DEER BALLS, DEER LOAF, AND ALL GROUND VENISON GOODIES IN BETWEEN!

By now you are probably thinking, "Wow! I can't believe I have survived this long without this great book!"

So far we have covered great recipes using deer burger in soups, chilies, casseroles, jerky, and sausage, and now I throw in the deer-cabin sink! But, first, I've got a little story for you.

Cousin Rick and Vinny were deer hunting when they came upon another hunter dragging a deer.

They both noticed how dang ugly the man was. In fact, the man was the ugliest person they had ever seen.

While talking to the man, they saw that he didn't have a gun. Cousin Rick said, "I see that you don't have a gun. Can I ask how it is that you managed to kill that buck?"

The ugly deer hunter said, "Well, I guess that you have noticed that I'm not very good looking."

They both admitted that they had noticed. The ugly hunter went on to say, "What I do is hide behind a tree and wait for a deer to come along and when he does, I peek around the tree. My face scares the deer so bad that it usually runs right into another tree and is struck dead."

Both Cousin Rick and Vinny were amazed at the man's story but believed him because he was just so darn ugly! Vinny says, "Wow that's amazing! Does anyone else in your family hunt like that too?"

The ugly hunter sighs and says. "Well, my wife used to come hunting with me, but she got to where she was just tearing them up too bad!"

Vickers Deer Balls

I pound deer burger
$^1/_2$ cup chopped green onion
$^1/_4$ cup flour
I egg
I teaspoon garlic salt
$^1/_2$ teaspoon white pepper
$^1/_4$ cup soy sauce
2 teaspoons cornstarch
$^1/_2$ cup water
I tablespoon cooking sherry
2 tablespoons brown sugar
$^1/_4$ teaspoon ginger
I tablespoon vegetable oil

In a large bowl, combine the meat, onion, flour, egg, garlic salt, pepper, soy sauce, cornstarch, water, sherry, brown sugar, and ginger.

Shape into deer balls. Heat the oil in a cast-iron skillet and cook until center is no longer pink.

Sloppy Does

2 pounds deer burger
I pound ground sausage
I chopped yellow onion
I cup ketchup
I cup vegetable juice
I cup shredded cheddar cheese
I teaspoon garlic salt
$^1/_2$ teaspoon white pepper

Heat oil in a large skillet; brown meat and onion, and drain off fat. Add the remaining ingredients, and simmer on low for about 45 minutes. Serve on burger buns.

My Favorite Deer Burger

I cup white wine
I cup minced white onion
$^1/_2$ cup chopped parsley
I teaspoon chervil
I teaspoon tarragon
I cup chicken broth
I cup unsalted butter
2 pounds deer burger
$^1/_2$ teaspoon garlic salt
$^1/_4$ teaspoon black pepper

In a saucepan, combine the wine, onions, parsley, chervil, and tarragon. Bring to a slow boil. Simmer on low heat until the mixture is about half reduced. Add the chicken broth, and keep simmering until you have about $^1/_2$ cup left in the pan. Cool, and set this mixture aside in a bowl.

Whip the butter until fluffy and soft. Add the whipped butter to the cool wine sauce, and lightly remix. Set the butter mixture covered in the refrigerator, and cool for 6 hours or more.

Mix the remaining ingredients together, and form deer burgers. Grill, and top the burgers with butter mixture.

Holland Grill BBQ Deer Burgers

3 pounds deer burger
$^1/_2$ cup minced onion
I teaspoon garlic salt
I teaspoon garlic powder
I cup chili sauce
2 tablespoons lemon juice
I cup ketchup
2 tablespoons brown sugar

In a large bowl, mix the deer burger, onion, and garlic salt together, and make into patties.

In another mixing bowl, add the remaining ingredients to make BBQ sauce. Brush sauce over patties while grilling. Grill the patties until no longer pink on the inside. Serve sauce with patties on buns.

Hunters on the Beach Burgers

I pound deer burger
2 tablespoons butter
I chopped onion
$^1/_2$ teaspoon cayenne pepper
$^1/_2$ teaspoon allspice
I teaspoon garlic salt
I teaspoon white pepper
I teaspoon curry powder
I teaspoon thyme
$^1/_2$ cup breadcrumbs
2 beaten brown eggs

In a large bowl, mix all the ingredients together, and form patties. Grill for about 6 minutes per side, and serve!

COUSIN RICK'S TOP FIVE SIGNS THAT YOUR GROUP HIRED THE WRONG DEER-HUNTING GUIDE

5. He blows into his homemade grunt call and a pack of wolves shows up.

4. He is completely outfitted with Scooby Doo camping equipment.

3. As you move in on your buck, he whispers in his Elmer Fudd voice, "Be vehhwey, vehhwey quiet."

2. Knows and calls all trees by their first and last names.

1. Just as you take aim with your bow, he starts screaming, "Run, Bambi, run!"

Mucho Mix

2 pounds deer burger
I chopped onion
¹/₄ cup bacon bits
I teaspoon garlic salt
I teaspoon cayenne pepper
I cup BBQ sauce
American cheese slices
Green bell pepper rings

In a large skillet, brown the deer burger and onion on medium heat until the burger is no longer pink, breaking up into ³/₄-inch crumbles. Pour off the drippings.

Stir in the remaining ingredients except the cheese and green bell pepper.

Spoon the cooked deer burger on buns, and top with the cheese and green bell pepper rings.

José Deer Burgers

I pound deer burger
I cup Mexican-style cheese
$^1/_2$ cup salsa
$^1/_4$ cup crushed tortilla chips
$^1/_2$ cup sliced green onions
I teaspoon chopped jalapeño peppers
I tablespoon cumin
$^1/_2$ teaspoon garlic salt
Sliced sourdough bread
Sliced tomatoes
Sliced lettuce

In a large bowl, combine deer burger, $^3/_4$ cup cheese, $^1/_4$ cup salsa, tortilla chips, sliced green onions, peppers, cumin, and garlic salt; mix together lightly. Shape into patties. Grill burgers until no longer pink in the center. Place buttered slices of sourdough bread on grill until golden brown. Place the grilled deer burgers on toasted bread; top with remaining cheese, salsa, tomatoes, and lettuce.

Al Capone Deer Tag Information Burgers

6 tablespoons dry breadcrumbs
$^1/_3$ cup chopped onions
$^1/_3$ cup chopped green bell pepper
I minced garlic clove
I teaspoon oregano
$^1/_2$ teaspoon garlic salt
$^1/_4$ teaspoon white pepper
I pound lean deer burger
6 tablespoons grated Parmesan cheese
15 ounces tomato sauce
I teaspoon Italian seasoning
Garlic toast slices

In a large bowl, combine the breadcrumbs, onions, green bell pepper, garlic, oregano, garlic salt, and pepper. Add deer burger and 3 tablespoons of the Parmesan cheese; mix well. Shape meat into patties. In a large cast-iron skillet, brown the deer patties for 3 minutes on each side. Combine the tomato sauce and Italian seasoning; pour over patties. Reduce heat and simmer for about 20 minutes on low heat.

Serve on toasted garlic toast topped with Parmesan cheese.

Campground Burgers

3 pounds deer burger
4 tablespoons garlic powder
4 tablespoons Worcestershire sauce
2 tablespoons black pepper
2 tablespoons onion flakes
2 tablespoons Tabasco sauce

In a large bowl, mix together all ingredients using your hands or a wooden spoon. Form into patties, and grill over campfire on cooking rack until no longer pink in the center.

Chicken Fried Venison

1 pound deer burger
$^1/_2$ cup milk
$^1/_2$ cup flour
$^1/_4$ cup oil
Salt and pepper to taste

Shape ground venison into patties, and chill. Place milk and flour in two flat dishes slightly larger than the venison patties. Place each venison patty in milk; turn over. Dip in flour. Place the coated venison patties in hot skillet with oil; season well. Cook on each side until golden and crispy, flattening as patties cook.

TRAVIS AT HUNTER'S SAFETY CLASS

Cousin Rick's boy, Travis, was at his hunter's safety class. The instructor picked Travis to answer a question about being lost in the timber. The instructor asked, "Travis Black, name three items that could save you should you become lost."

Travis confidently answered, "A compass, water, and a deck of cards."

"Explain your answers," the instructor said.

Travis replied, "The compass could be used to find my way. The water would prevent dehydration."

"What about the cards?" the instructor demanded.

"Well, sir, as soon as I'd start playing solitaire, my dad is bound to come up behind me and say, 'Put that red nine on top of that black ten!'"

Lazy Buck Rolls

I pound deer burger
I pound ground pork
2 chopped onions
2 cups rice
I teaspoon garlic salt with parsley
$^1\!/_2$ teaspoon pepper
I shredded cabbage head
10 ounces tomato soup

Fry the deer burger, pork, and onions together until brown. Cover the rice with boiling water, add salt and pepper, and then boil until water is absorbed. Fry the cabbage until limp. Mix all the ingredients together in a large baking dish, and cover with the tomato soup. Bake in a 350-degree oven for 30 minutes.

Venison Venioganoff

I pound deer burger
I egg
$^3\!/_4$ cup soft breadcrumbs
$^1\!/_4$ cup water
I teaspoon salt
$^1\!/_2$ teaspoon white pepper
I teaspoon oil
10 ounces mushroom soup
$^1\!/_2$ cup water
2 tablespoons ketchup
I tablespoon minced onion
I tablespoon Worcestershire sauce
$^1\!/_2$ teaspoon garlic powder
$^1\!/_2$ cup sour cream

Combine deer burger, egg, breadcrumbs, $^1\!/_4$ cup water, salt, and pepper. Form into small meatballs; brown on all sides in the oil. Drain off all fat, and push the meatballs to one side of the kettle. Add the soup, $^1\!/_2$ cup water, ketchup, onions, Worcestershire sauce, and garlic powder. Mix well, and simmer on low heat for about 5 minutes. Mix in the sour cream, and simmer for another 4 minutes. Serve over rice or noodles.

Becky's Wild Muffin

2 tablespoons butter
$^1/_2$ pound sliced mushrooms
$^1/_2$ cup chopped onions
$^1/_2$ teaspoon thyme
$^1/_2$ teaspoon garlic salt
1 pound deer burger, shaped into patties
Buttered and toasted English muffins

In a large cast-iron skillet, melt butter and sauté mushrooms, onion, thyme, and garlic salt until the onions are tender.

Set the onions aside, but keep them warm. Fry the deer burger patties in skillet until no longer pink in the center. Serve deer burgers on muffins topped with onion mixture.

Muzzleloader Rice

1 pound deer burger
1 tablespoon olive oil
$1/2$ cup chopped yellow onion
1 teaspoon seasoning salt
$1/2$ teaspoon white pepper
$1/4$ teaspoon freshly ground black pepper
$1/2$ teaspoon thyme
$1/2$ teaspoon garlic powder
$1/2$ teaspoon oregano
12 ounces canned mushrooms
12 ounces tomato sauce
1 cup milk
1 cup cooked rice
$1/2$ cup cheddar cheese

In a large cast-iron skillet, cook the venison, olive oil, onion, seasoning salt, white pepper, black pepper, thyme, garlic powder, and oregano. Drain any remaining fat when done. After draining off fat, add the mushrooms, tomato sauce, milk, cooked rice, and cheese to the burger in pan.

Simmer, stirring often, and serve hot!

Timber to the Table Venison Roast

3 pounds deer burger
1 cup cream of celery soup
$1/4$ cup canned mushrooms
$1/2$ cup water
$1/2$ teaspoon seasoning salt
$1/4$ teaspoon cayenne pepper
1 package dry onion soup

In a large mixing bowl, combine all the ingredients together, and mix well using your hands. Line a baking dish with foil, and coat with cooking spray. Make a loaf from venison mixture. Place the loaf onto the coated foil, and wrap top of loaf with foil, making a tight seal. Bake at 300 degrees for about 3 hours, or until the loaf is no longer pink in the center.

BEFORE THE HUNT CHECKLIST

Are you ready for the hunt? I can't count how many times I found myself a long way from civilization without something critically important, like the right gloves so that my fingers weren't too cold to pull off that one second shot, or I'd forgotten to pack extra socks or a pair of sneakers so I didn't have to walk around camp wearing my muddy hunting boots. To help you learn from my mistakes, I've put together a checklist of things to remember to make hunting life a tad bit better.

Hunting Equipment
☐ Weapon/ammo
☐ Game calls
☐ Knife
☐ Fanny pack
☐ Camera/film/video camera
☐ Binoculars
☐ Bone saw
☐ Nylon rope
☐ Canteen/water bottle
☐ Flashlight/extra batteries
☐ Cell phone
☐ Tags/I.D.
☐ Gas cans/fuel
☐ First aid/survival kit
☐ Stand safety belt
☐ Two-way radios
☐ Cover/masking sprays

Clothing
☐ Extra socks
☐ Rain gear
☐ Boots
☐ Sneakers/cabin shoes
☐ Gloves
☐ Extra tops/bottoms
☐ Blaze orange coverage
☐ Gun belt
☐ Face mask
☐ Hand/boot warmers
☐ Eyeglass/scope towel
☐ Toilet paper/clean wipes
☐ Hunting jackets/coats
☐ Bibs (noninsulated and insulated)

This is *not* a complete checklist, but it will get you started in making a list of all the items that are important to you. Remember the little things: a watch so you can meet your party at a certain time, your medications, and insect repellent. Always check and recheck all your hunting camp/cabin gear before leaving home. Remember to check all family members' gear also (speaking from experience).

Slow Cooker Venison Loaf

2 pounds deer burger
I chopped yellow onion
20 crushed cheese-flavored saltines
2 tablespoons minced green bell pepper
$1/4$ cup chili sauce
$1/2$ cup milk
2 beaten brown eggs
I teaspoon seasoning salt
$1/2$ teaspoon cayenne pepper

In a large bowl, mix together all ingredients. Form into an 8-inch round loaf. Place loaf in a slow cooker, cover, and cook on low for about 8 hours, or turn on the slow cooker at the beginning of the hunt and eat that night back at the cabin.

Peppers Stuffed with Deer

2 pounds deer burger
2 cups shredded mozzarella cheese
Red bell peppers
I package Cajun-style rice
I teaspoon cayenne pepper
I teaspoon hot sauce

Preheat the oven to 350 degrees. Cut the tops out of the red peppers, and clean the seeds out. Put the peppers in a large pot, and boil until tender.

Cook the rice according to the package instructions. Brown, and drain the deer burger. Mix the deer burger, rice, seasonings, and 1 cup of cheese.

Place the peppers in a baking dish sprayed with cooking oil. Spoon the deer burger and rice mixture into the peppers. Place remaining cheese on top of meat in peppers. Bake for about 30 minutes.

Note: For even greater flavor, add $1/4$ cup beer to baking dish before baking.

Sharpshooter Sandwiches

A Deer Cabin Classic

2 pounds deer burger
1 pound whole hog sausage
1 teaspoon minced garlic
$^1/_2$ teaspoon seasoning salt
$^1/_4$ teaspoon pepper
1 package Cheez Whiz
1 loaf sliced pumpernickel bread

In a large cast-iron skillet, cook together the deer burger, sausage, garlic, seasoning salt, and pepper. Drain off all fat, and add the Cheez Whiz. Simmer on low for about 5 minutes. Place deer burger and cheese mixture onto bread slices, and bake for about 20 minutes in a 350-degree oven. Serve hot.

Hunters' Supper "Foiled" By Deer Again!

Another great meal used by our hunting party.

2 pounds deer burger, cooked and crumbled
1 pound smoked bacon, cooked and in bits
1 small can of canned milk
1 egg
$^1/_2$ cup chopped white onion
1 tablespoon mustard
2 teaspoons garlic salt
1 teaspoon Accent
1 teaspoon white pepper
2 cups American cheese
1 loaf French bread

Combine the cooked deer burger, bacon bits, milk, egg, onion, mustard, garlic salt, Accent, white pepper, and cheese in a large mixing bowl, and mix well using a large spoon.

Spread the mixture on halved bread loaves; wrap foil around bottom and sides of bread, leaving the meat mixture unwrapped and exposed to heat. Bake at 350 degrees for about 20 minutes. Serve slices hot.

Deer 'N' Cheese Vittles

I pound deer burger
I teaspoon salt
¹/₂ teaspoon black pepper
¹/₄ teaspoon cumin
I chopped green bell pepper
I cup chopped onion
I2 ounces canned corn, drained
I6 ounces canned tomatoes, diced, with juice
6 ounces tomato paste
I package macaroni and cheese, prepared as package directs

Brown the deer burger with seasonings in a large cast-iron skillet. Add the onion and green pepper; continue cooking until the onion is tender. Add the corn, tomatoes, and tomato paste; simmer for about 5 minutes on low heat.

Stir in the prepared macaroni and cheese and simmer all for about 10 minutes.

TELLIN' IT LIKE IT IS

"I'm so ashamed of the way we live," a young wife said to her lazy husband, who refused to get a job and instead just hunted and fished all the time.

"My daddy pays our rent. My momma buys all the food. My sister buys all our clothes. My uncle gave us a truck. I'm so ashamed!"

The husband glared over his beer at her as he thumbed through his hunting catalog, "You should be ashamed," he agreed.

"Those two worthless brothers of yours never give us a cent!"

Buckeye Buns

1 pound deer burger
$^1/_2$ cup chopped onion
8 ounces tomato soup
1 cup chopped black and green olives, mixed
$^1/_2$ cup mayonnaise
$^1/_4$ cup mushrooms
$^1/_2$ teaspoon oregano
$^1/_4$ teaspoon black pepper
$^1/_4$ teaspoon garlic salt
$^1/_2$ pound grated mozzarella cheese
8 hamburger buns

In a large skillet, brown the deer burger with onion, and drain fat. Let the meat and onion mixture cool. Mix the remaining ingredients with the cooled deer burger mixture.

Put on halved hamburger buns. Bake for 25 minutes in a 300-degree oven. Serve hot.

Calvary Toast

2 pounds deer burger
1 chopped white onion
2 sliced celery stalks
1 teaspoon minced garlic
2 beef bouillon cubes
1 cup beef stock
$^1/_4$ cup soy sauce

In a large skillet, brown the deer burger, onion, and celery until the veggies are tender and no pink is showing in meat. Drain fat, and add the bouillon cubes, beef stock, soy sauce, and minced garlic. Simmer for about 10 minutes on low heat, stirring often. Serve venison and gravy over toast.

Hash Fer Hicks

1 pound deer burger
1 chopped onion
1 pound diced potatoes
3 tablespoons beef bouillon
$^1/_2$ teaspoon salt
$^1/_4$ teaspoon white pepper

Brown the deer burger and onion in a large saucepan until meat is no longer pink. Add the potatoes, bouillon, salt, pepper, and water to cover. Cover the saucepan, lower heat, and let simmer for about 35 minutes, or until the potatoes are tender and the water has reduced.

Ranch-Style Hunter's Hash

1 pound deer burger
4 cups frozen O'Brien-style potatoes
11 ounces canned Mexican-style corn, undrained
$^3/_4$ cup water
1 beef bouillon cube
$^1/_2$ teaspoon cumin
Salt and pepper to taste
1 tablespoon diced parsley

Brown the venison burger in a large skillet over medium heat until thoroughly cooked, and drain off any remaining fat.

Add all the remaining ingredients except the salt, pepper, and parsley; mix well. Reduce the heat to low; cover, and cook for about 25 minutes, or until the potatoes are tender, stirring often. Season with salt and pepper to taste. Sprinkle with the parsley.

Midwestern Deer Dip

I pound deer burger, browned and drained
I pound Velveeta cheese
I can chili with beans
$^1/_4$ cup dark beer
15 ounces salsa with jalapeños

In a large slow cooker, mix in the cooked deer burger, cheese, chili with beans, beer, and salsa with jalapeños.

Heat mixture until the cheese is very soft, and the mixture can be dipped with a corn chip. Keep on low heat, and enjoy with your favorite corn chips.

YOU'RE A TRUE COUSIN RICK FAN IF . . .

You love the outdoors.

You love having fun with friends and family.

You love cooking and swapping wild-game recipes.

You do your part in supporting conservation clubs.

You take time out to teach our young ones the joys of outdoor sports.

And you promise to follow the 10 Commandments of Firearm Safety!

1. Always keep the muzzle pointed in a safe direction.
2. Treat every firearm as though it were loaded.
3. Unload firearm, open action except when ready to shoot.
4. Keep barrel clear, and choose the proper ammunition for the firearm.
5. Be sure of your target before you pull the trigger.
6. Never point a firearm at anything you don't want to shoot.
7. Never climb or jump with a loaded firearm.
8. Never shoot at a flat, hard surface or water.
9. Store firearms and ammunition separately.
10. Avoid alcohol and drugs before and during shooting.

If you share one thing from this book, share this!

Your old cousin Rick has a few more recipes, tips, and jokes he wants to share with you . . .

Deer Balls Loose in Kansas City Dish

1 pound deer burger
1 minced onion
$^1/_2$ cup breadcrumbs
1 teaspoon garlic salt
$^1/_2$ teaspoon white pepper
1 egg
Milk
2 tablespoons oil
$^3/_4$ cup ketchup
$^1/_3$ cup Kansas City-style beer
3 tablespoons Dijon mustard
2 tablespoons brown sugar
1 tablespoon Worcestershire sauce

In a large bowl, combine the deer burger, onion, breadcrumbs, garlic salt, pepper, egg, and a little milk to moisten. Make into meatballs and in a large skillet, cook in hot oil. Remove meatballs with tongs or a slotted spoon. After removing, add the ketchup, beer, mustard, brown sugar, and Worcestershire sauce to the skillet, and bring to a boil.

Return the deer meatballs to the sauce in the skillet, and simmer all until hot.

Hobo Hunter Deer Delight

2 pounds deer burger
2 bags frozen vegetables
1 teaspoon garlic powder
$^1/_2$ teaspoon white pepper
$^1/_2$ teaspoon salt
4 tablespoons butter

Roll out a large piece of foil, and spray with cooking oil. Place the deer burger and frozen vegetables on foil. Season with the garlic powder, pepper, and salt. Top with butter slices, and cover mixture with another large piece of foil.

Double- or triple-wrap with another piece of foil. Poke five small holes on each side of wrapped mixture, and place on a grill.

Grill each side for about 40 minutes each.

6

MEALS
FOR A
LARGE CROWD

STOP! KATIE BAR THE DOOR!

A fellow committee member of one of the many conservation clubs I belong to called to ask what I had on the menu for our upcoming Wild Game Feed. After informing him of my cooking plans, I thought, "Wow, why not give my readers four of my favorite venison recipes that feed over a hundred people so they can use them for their Wild Game Feeds!"

I know what you're thinking. This is the best venison cookbook. You're right!

Salem Stub Wild and Sloppy Joe Hunters

Serves 250

50 pounds deer burger
3 cups finely chopped onions
8 cups finely chopped celery
$^1/_4$ cup dry mustard
$^1/_2$ cup brown sugar
I cup vinegar
4 large cans tomato soup
6 tablespoons salt
6 tablespoons black pepper
5 tablespoons garlic powder
21 dozen hamburger buns

In a very large pot or kettle, fry venison and onions. Drain. Combine the remaining ingredients in a 6-gallon pot. Simmer for about an hour and serve on buns.

Hunters Who Be Hungry Loaf

Serves 120

40 pounds deer burger
16 eggs, lightly beaten
8 cups oatmeal
5 cups vegetable juice
4 chopped yellow onions
$1/3$ cup seasoning salt
3 tablespoons black pepper
3 cups water
2 cups ketchup
7 tablespoons vinegar
3 tablespoons yellow mustard
2 tablespoons brown sugar

Combine the first seven ingredients, and shape into 16 loaves. Place into loaf pans. Combine the remaining ingredients, and pour about 3 tablespoons over each loaf. Bake at 350 degrees for about 90 minutes, or until the meat is thoroughly cooked with no pink showing. Baste once with the remaining sauce while cooking.

Cousin Rick's Feed Your Army Wild Game Breakfast

Serves about 120 hungry hunters

15 pounds deer burger
3 pounds chopped bacon
4 chopped onions
2 chopped green bell peppers
2 cups sliced canned mushrooms
1 chopped red bell pepper
100 eggs
10 cups milk
2 teaspoons nonfat dry milk
2 teaspoons lemon juice
4 tablespoons salt
2 pounds butter

In a large pot, cook the deer burger, bacon, onions, green bell pepper, mushrooms, and red bell pepper. Break eggs into a large, clean mixing bowl. Beat slightly on medium speed. Combine with milk, nonfat dry milk, lemon juice, and salt.

Drain deer burger mixture, and add to egg mixture. Melt butter, and divide equally into steam-table pans. Bake in a preheated 350-degree oven for about 45 minutes, stirring occasionally.

Wildghetti Sauce

Sauce will serve a mountain of spaghetti

20 pounds deer burger, cooked and drained
20 minced garlic cloves
320 ounces canned tomatoes, chopped, with juice
22 tablespoons parsley
15 bay leaves, in cheesecloth
10 teaspoons garlic salt
15 teaspoons oregano
10 teaspoons brown sugar
3 teaspoons thyme
60 ounces tomato paste
10 cups minced onions
2 cups chopped green peppers
18 stalks chopped celery
7 cups water
3 cups beer

In a very large kettle, add all the ingredients, and simmer on low, uncovered, for about 4 hours, stirring every 10 minutes with a large spoon. When the sauce is done, remove bay leaves in cheesecloth.

INDEX

·